"Through vivid stories of his own experiences and those of the people he counsels, Dr. Wright breaks down the differences in how men and women communicate and then teaches us how to bridge the gap. This is a much-needed resource that gives invaluable information on a new way of connecting and sharing with your spouse, no matter how long you have been together. The Energy Builders at the end of each chapter are especially helpful in putting this new way of communicating into practice."

—Eric and Jennifer Garcia, cofounders,
Association of Marriage and Family Ministries

"Norm has the rare ability to write in a very relaxed and comfortable style, making you feel as if he is sitting in a chair in your family room talking with you. At the same time, he communicates deeply and intuitively regarding the problems many couples have in sharing thoughts, emotions, and feelings with each other, and how they can effectively resolve these problems. We heartily recommend the reading of this book to any couple searching for deeper and more powerfully healing relationships with each other."

—Drs. Tom and Beverly Rodgers, authors, speakers,
and marriage and family therapists, Charlotte, NC

"What we have here is a failure to communicate! Not anymore. Communication is the lifeblood of every relationship, and Dr. Wright's is the right book to help you bridge the communication gap in your marriage. If you want to deepen your intimacy and connect in meaningful ways, read this book."

—Ron L. Deal, president, Successful Stepfamilies.com,
and marriage and family therapist

"When my car breaks down, I don't try to tinker with it on my own. I call in a professional who understands the mechanics of how the car works. Likewise, when communication breaks down in a marriage, it makes sense to call in a professional who understands the mechanics of how a husband and wife keep their relationship on track. If you and your spouse have experienced a breakdown on the road of your marriage, if you feel as if you just can't seem to understand each other, I strongly suggest you call in the expert, Norm Wright. Norm has gotten his hands dirty for over thirty years helping couples who have hit a bump in the road in their journey toward marital happiness. In HOW TO SPEAK YOUR SPOUSE'S LANGUAGE, he breaks down the mechanics of speaking to and listening to and thinking about the one you love so that your marriage can become the joy ride you've always wanted."

—Nancy Guthrie, author of
Holding On to Hope and *The One Year Book of Hope*

"In the forest of books on marriage relationships, this one stands tall. I've read literally hundreds of books on relationships and this is one is unique. If you feel frustrated, stuck, or discouraged in your marriage, this book will be a refreshing breath of hope and help. It is packed with suggestions that have been forged in real-life experiences. If you are tired of pie-in-the-sky platitudes or superficial solutions, this book will give you practical ways to connect at the deepest levels. Buy it, read it, apply it, and watch your marriage go to the next level."

—Gary J. Oliver, PhD, executive director of
The Center for Relationship Enrichment, John Brown University, and
coauthor of *Raising Sons and Loving It!* and
A Woman's Forbidden Emotion

"If it is your desire to respectfully and intelligently enter the world of 'another,' if you want to up your chance of being heard and of having a hearing, let H. Norman Wright be your guide into the fascinating and rewarding domain of effective communication. Apply the principles in this book and you will revolutionize your communication."

—Dr. David and Janet Congo, coauthors of
One Good Year of Marriage:
Making the Most of the Rest of Your Marriage
and founders of eLifeMates

"Norm Wright did it again! A solid book for real couples who want to talk in a way so their spouses will listen, not only to their words, but also to their hearts. Norm gets to the heart of what complicates couples' communication. He outlines the fine nuances of a couple's conversation and shows how a couple can talk and really be heard. I am going to make this a must-read for all the couples I counsel, as well as the counselors I train. Norm has spent years in the counseling room; he knows what he is talking about, and it shows."

—Sharon Hart (Morris) May, PhD, coauthor of *Safe Haven Marriage:*
How to Build a Relationship You Want to Come Home To
and originator of Haven of Safety Marriage Intensives

"This book will help you really connect with your mate, because it shows you why that so often does not happen and what you can do to make a difference. It's warm, it's clear—it's Norm Wright."

—Scott Stanley, author of *The Power of Commitment*

"When it comes to communication in marriage, H. Norman Wright wrote the book. Read it—and find the satisfaction in your marriage that you've always wanted."

—Dr. Greg Smalley, The Center for Relationship Enrichment,
John Brown University, and coauthor of *The DNA of Relationships*

HOW TO
SPEAK YOUR
Spouse's
LANGUAGE

*Ten Easy Steps to Great
Communication from One of America's
Foremost Counselors*

H. NORMAN WRIGHT

**CENTER
STREET®**

NEW YORK   BOSTON   NASHVILLE

Center Street
Hachette Book Group USA
1271 Avenue of the Americas, New York, NY 10020
Visit our Web site at www.centerstreet.com

Center Street® is a division of Hachette Book Group USA.
The Center Street name and logo are trademarks of Hachette Book Group USA.
Printed in the United States of America
First Edition: November 2006
10 9 8 7 6 5 4 3 2 1

Library of Congress Cataloging-in-Publication Data
Wright, H. Norman.
    How to speak your spouse's language : ten easy steps to great communication /
from one of America's foremost counselors H. Norman Wright. — 1st ed.
        p. cm.
    ISBN-13: 978-1-59995-682-4
    ISBN-10: 1-59995-682-9
    1. Communication in marriage—United States. 2. Interpersonal relations. I. Title.

HQ734.W94919 2006
646.7'8—dc22   2006015076

Contents

Contents

How to Speak Your Spouse's Language

1

Do You Speak the Same Language?
STEP #1: BE AN IMMIGRANT—DIVE INTO FOREIGN SOIL!

It was hard not to notice the young couple sitting at the restaurant table. They were looking at each other with rapt attention and it was obvious a strong chemistry was brewing. The noise from other tables didn't distract them. They talked together as though they were the only couple there.

As he spoke, her facial expression showed that she devoured every word. When she responded, he nodded in agreement, raised his eyebrows on occasion, and looked intently into her face as she shared with him. The depth of their personal attention to each other indicated a couple very much in love.

A man at a nearby table observed them. As they finished their dinner conversation and got up to leave, he stopped them. "Pardon me," he said. "Could I ask you a question?"

They stopped and smiled. "Of course. What is it?"

"I couldn't help but notice the two of you talking together," the man replied. "You both seemed to be hanging on each other's every word. Do you feel you can communicate so you really know what the other person means? Are you really able to grasp what your partner feels and believes? Do you—"

The couple interrupted him with laughter. "Of course we do," the woman said. "There's absolutely no problem in the way we communicate. We're on the same wavelength. That's one of the reasons we're so attracted to each other. Communication is *no* problem for us!"

Two weeks later the couple walked down the aisle of their church and committed themselves to each other for life, and they communicated happily ever after. *Or did they?*

Five years later, same restaurant, same couple, same man seated at a corner table, watching this couple talk: They speak but don't communicate. They interrupt each other, shaking their heads or rolling their eyes in disgust. At times they look angry. The husband glances around the room as the wife continues to talk to him. She raises her hands in a frustrated manner, and her voice begins to carry to adjacent tables. He shakes his head, and his eyes convey unbelief and confusion. Soon they leave their table and begin walking out of the restaurant.

The man observing intercepts them and asks, "May I ask you a question?"

The couple stop, hesitate, and look at each other and then back at the man with puzzled expressions.

The husband responds, "Well . . . all right. What's your question?"

"It's very simple," the man replies. Then he repeats the questions he asked five years earlier. "I couldn't help but notice you talking. Do you feel you can communicate so that you really know what the other person means? Are you really able to grasp what your partner feels and believes? Do you—"

The wife interrupts the man, exclaiming, "Communicate! I try, but he doesn't listen. Either his mind is fried, or he doesn't have the capacity to understand simple language. You'd think I was talking to a stranger. And—"

Her husband breaks in. "Half the time I don't even understand what she's trying to say. You'd think she's speaking a different language. We can't communicate! We talk past each other. I'm on AM, but she's on FM. She sees things so differently from the way I do. And she talks incessantly. On and on and on! I don't know what she's trying to say."

They begin arguing and the man quietly slips into the background as the couple walks away, each oblivious to the fact that neither is listening. Years ago they thought they could communicate, but now. . . .

MEET SHERI AND FRED

Let's consider another couple—Sheri and Fred. They've been married for twenty-two years. Sheri says:

> After I married Fred, the relationship was okay. But then I felt pinned down or restricted by him. He is so mechanical and precise, he takes the fun out of everything. It's as though we both look at the world and even though we stand in the same place, we see something different.
>
> Fred seems to have a clipboard and is making a list of the facts. It's one thing to be literal, but he is extreme. I know I'm not always the most practical, but Fred is overly so . . . and "realistic"—at least that's the way he sees himself. I love possibilities and speculation, but he doesn't seem to see the value of either.
>
> We have so many arguments over my answers. He'd ask, "What time will you be getting home?" and I'd say, "Around five o'clock." That wouldn't do it for him. He needed to know the exact time. If I buy something, it isn't enough that I tell him it was around forty dollars. He wants to know it to the penny.
>
> For several years he wouldn't ask me for directions anywhere—I mean *anywhere*—even inside a building.

Fred wants a detailed, step-by-step map. I can find where I'm going with instructions like "It's a couple of blocks or signals down Seventeenth and you'll pass some kind of a school on the left, then in a little while you'll turn right and the store is, uh, let's see, two or three blocks on the right. Oh, you can't miss it." That's not good enough for Fred. He says it's not precise enough.

The future intrigues me much more than what's going on at the present time. There are all sorts of surprises to be discovered. Fred looks at things today and wants to know if they work or not. I'd rather think of the possibilities.

Whenever we buy something that needs to be put together, Fred can't wait to get back into the box and find the instructions. He loves to follow them exactly. A friend of mine asked me to think of a word that would describe Fred. The first word that came to mind was *predictable*. I could set the clock by him. I can tell you what time he gets up, leaves the house, and what he has for lunch. He'll drive the same streets to work or the gym, even though we've got several options.

You can imagine what our communication is like. I don't have the same problem with some of my other friends. But at least I always know the subject we're talking about when Fred brings it up—he identifies it precisely.

This is Fred's story:

Someone asked me what attracted me to Sheri. Excitement! My life was fairly routine. She brought a lot of fun into my life. But after we married, it seemed to get old in a hurry. She seemed scattered and going in several directions at once. She was always looking for some new possibility.

When we plan a vacation, it really doesn't start for me until we get there. But for Sheri, it seems to start as soon as we mention it. She loves the unknown. And when she describes what we did and where we went, her perceptions are so different from mine that I wonder if we were on the same vacation. The word *exactness* isn't in her vocabulary. I ask her for something and I hear, "It's over there somewhere." It's as if she's talking a different language.

When I ask a simple question, all I want is a simple, clear, concise answer, not a hundred possibilities. She takes longer and puts things in a different order. That drives me up a wall.

She says I nitpick, but I think she takes an incident and blows it way out of proportion. It's amazed me for years how she and the women friends who are just like her can carry on a conversation. They start a sentence and never finish it but jump to another one and don't finish that before jumping to the next and the next. And yet, they seem to understand each other. I've tried. I mean I've tried, but it's beyond me. I learned to say, "Sheri, I want to hear what you have to say, and it helps me if you could condense it and finish a sentence before going on. I'll stick with you better." At least that worked.

I've learned that Sheri's mind and body might be two different places. We could be watching a movie together and I'm really into it, but I'll ask her a question and she's thinking about something else.

We have different definitions for words such as "No," "Later," "Sometimes," and "I'll get it done."

LANGUAGE BARRIERS IN BUSINESS — AND THE LIVING ROOM

The problem isn't limited to married couples. Let's listen in on two people discussing a business deal.

> *George:* I don't understand it. I worked and worked on the proposal for weeks. I did my homework, covered every angle, and made what I thought was a great presentation.
>
> *Frank:* Well, what happened then? Why did they go for the competitor's proposal?
>
> *George:* I can't figure it out. It's got me stumped. Especially since I have a copy of the other company's bid. It's no different from ours. In fact, we came in a bit lower in cost. I don't understand it.
>
> *Frank:* There's got to be a reason. How did your presentation go?
>
> *George:* I felt it went well. It didn't take long. They didn't ask many questions. I made it very clear, and they seemed polite and interested. I thought I had it sewed up. I was so sure I had it, I waited around until after our competitor's presentation. I thought they would want to sign then.
>
> *Frank:* Why? What made you think they were ready?
>
> *George:* The other presentation was three times as long. It was complicated and confusing. I don't know why they spent so much time in there. I was sure we were on the same wavelength, and they would go with us.

But George was *not* on the same wavelength with his audience when he made the presentation. Oh, what he presented was good, but he failed to connect with his listeners. Why? *Because he wasn't speaking their language!* They were much more comfortable with the other person's presentation, and a rapport was established. That's why they signed.

A husband and wife sit in their softly lit family room, listening to the sounds of an orchestra coming from the stereo. The room is comfortable and a few pleasant smells from dinner linger in the air. They sit across from each other, looking at the plans for remodeling one section of their home.

Bob: If you'll look over the new design and room arrangement, you can't help but see that I've focused on the suggestions that you mentioned the last time we looked these over. I just can't see what's bothering you about these changes now.

Jean: I don't know. I just keep getting the feeling that something in this room is missing. I can't define it. We need to get a better handle on something.

Bob: I think you're just stuck in your own point of view. You remember something from your home when you were a kid, and you'd like to see it here. Look at it from a different perspective. Then you'll see how this arrangement will be so much better than what you're talking about.

Jean: No. I don't think you have the proper feel for what this room can express. You need to get in touch with this arrangement from my point of view. Don't you understand what I'm telling you?

What do you think? Will they understand each other? Or are they speaking two different languages? Think about it. Read it again. Do you catch the difference in their words? (Chapter 8 will explain this.)

Two college students are talking over dinner. One says, "You know, I really feel comfortable talking with the new college dean. What a difference between him and the old one. This guy understands me. I can just tell it. We really seem to speak the same language."

His friend replies, "Yeah, I know what you're saying. He

shows an interest and lets you know that he's really tuning into you. He *does* seem to speak our language."

There it is!

There *what* is? One of the greatest secrets of effective communication and conversation. Follow this principle, and you'll be amazed at the results: *Speak the same language as the other person!*

What does *that* mean? Am I saying you should find people who talk in the same manner you do—that these are the only ones you can really communicate with? *No*, I don't mean that at all. That would limit you to a select few. Instead I'd like to show you how to be flexible and learn the language of those with whom you come in contact. That allows you to effectively communicate with almost everyone.

COMMUNICATION AND A FOREIGN LANGUAGE

Have you ever traveled in a foreign country? There are two types of travelers: the colonizer and the immigrant. The colonizer wants to visit another country but sees it from his own perspective instead of experiencing it from the inhabitants' point of view. As he enters the country, he looks for signs in his own language and seeks out people who speak his own tongue. He endeavors to find the familiar and fails to venture into uncharted territory. He doesn't branch out and learn any words in this foreign language.

In fact, this traveler becomes irritated when he can't read signs for the bathroom or understand the menu. Instead of asking for help or learning a few helpful phrases, he becomes upset. He's dependent on others from his country who can interpret for him and guide him around. When he talks to local residents, he approaches them in his own language. They either respond with puzzlement or say a few words they've learned and point him in some direction.

Our traveler ends up creating an unpleasant experience for himself and can't wait to get back to familiar territory. He returns home with the attitude that people in that country aren't very friendly. They weren't interested or helpful. If they had been, they would have provided messages in his language and learned his language in order to help tourism.

Quite often colonizing nations do this. They transport their own language, customs, and monetary system to another country and force the people there to become like them.

The immigrant traveler is different. He's somewhat of an adventurer. He prepares for his trip in advance by orienting himself to this foreign culture. He reads books about the culture, customs, and history of the country and attempts to learn everyday phrases of this new language. In order to converse with the native population, he may even take a class in their language before he leaves. When he arrives at his destination, he's eager to discover all he can. He looks for historical sites, tries all the new foods, reads as much as he can in the language of the country, and uses his newly formed verbal skills where possible. He may even enjoy living with a family of that country for a while in order to fully capture the flavor of this new world.

As the immigrant attempts to speak this new language, the people respond in a helpful manner. They help him pronounce strange words. Often, if they're adept in the traveler's language, they'll begin to speak it in order to make *him* feel more comfortable. They seem delighted that this person has made an attempt to learn their language, and both of them can laugh at some of his mispronunciations. When the immigrant returns home, he's bursting with enthusiasm and stories of his experiences. He says the people were so friendly, so open, and so interesting. They were delightful.

But wait a minute! Both the colonizer and the immigrant went to the same country. They encountered the same people. Why the difference in response? Simple. The immigrant was willing to learn about the culture of the people and to speak their language. As he attempted to speak the way they did, the people responded positively to his attempts and tried to make it easier for him by speaking his language in return.

I'm reminded of a cross-cultural snapshot one of my friends described to me. On a brief trip to Haiti, he found himself alone in a room with a young Haitian man who seemed wide-eyed with excitement about meeting an American. The Haitian obviously longed to open a conversation. His hands opened and closed. His eyes burned with a desire to weave his thoughts into understandable words. He seemed to have a thousand questions on the tip of his tongue. But my friend didn't speak a word of Creole and the Haitian didn't speak English. So eventually, after a few smiles, nods, vague gestures, and self-conscious shrugs, the two men strolled awkwardly to different corners of the room, and they parted almost certainly for the rest of their lives.

That little experience paints a powerful analogy in my mind. You and I know men and women who live together ten, twenty, *fifty* years or more but never learn to speak one another's language. They sit in rooms together, ride in cars together, eat meals together, take vacations together, and sleep together when the sun goes down. But for year after empty year, they never learn how to get beyond vague gestures and a few surface phrases.

Yes, it's true that many couples speak a language that's different in structure, style, and meaning, which can result in "crossed wires" or mixed messages.

Don't worry, though. This isn't a fatal condition. It is just a matter of "rewiring" or learning about your spouse's language style. This can make the difference between marital health and marital anguish. Seldom do husband and wife have the same language, but they can learn a new one. Remember, you can't rely on your native tongue if your spouse doesn't speak the same language.

So, if you really want to communicate, don't put the responsibility on the other person to understand you. Reach out and attempt to understand the other person first, and that will free him up to respond to you.

How can you do this? In this book I'll provide you with the principles for effective communication. They're simple. And they work. If the way you're communicating isn't working, what have you got to lose by trying a new method? If you feel your communication *is* working, let's make it even *more* effective.

One last question: what are you—a colonizer or an immigrant?

"Speak my language and I'll respond to you."

ENERGY BUILDERS

1. Describe a situation in which you experienced difficulty communicating. What happened? What could have been done differently?
2. If you have ever traveled to a foreign country, reflect on your communication experiences. What could have made them better?
3. What will you do this week with the information in this chapter? Describe how your communication will be different.

2

What Are You Trying to Say?
Step #2: Make the Most of Verbal and
Nonverbal Communication

You're at a social gathering with a group of friends. You're listening to a newcomer talk on and on. During a lull in the conversation, two of you excuse yourselves, and as you walk away you ask, "Did you understand what he was trying to say?" Your friend replies with a laugh, "No. I'm not even sure that *he* knew what he was trying to say!"

An uncommon occurrence? No! People talk without knowing for sure what they want to get across. Their purpose is clouded, and their presentation leaves the listener confused and perplexed. I've experienced both sides of this problem. On occasion I've wondered what the other individual or speaker is trying to get across, and at other times, I've caused others to wonder what I really wanted to say.

Perhaps some of the problems in communication can be seen in this exchange. Imagine a couple coming to a counselor because they are at the point of getting a divorce. The counselor asks the wife, "Does your husband beat you up?"

She answers, "No, I beat him up by several hours every morning."

Then the counselor asks the husband, "Do you hold a grudge?"

The husband responds, "No, we have a carport."

The exasperated counselor asks the couple, "What grounds do you have for your problems?"

The wife answers, "We have about four acres."

Finally, the counselor asks, "Why did you come here today?"

Together they say, "We can't seem to communicate."

RULES FOR CLEAR COMMUNICATION

Following a few basic communication principles can change the process.

Know When Something Needs to Be Said and Say It Straight

This means you don't assume that other people know what you think, feel, want, or need. Communication should be clear and direct. If anything, assume the other knows very little about what you're going to say and that you need to make it clear— even when you're married to the other person! None of us can attend a school for mind reading. We're all failures at being clairvoyant. I have heard people say, "We've been married for twenty years. Why should I have to tell her . . . ?" "He should know how much that hurts." Or "It was so obvious. Why should anyone have to express it?" Obvious to whom? Clearly not to the other party.

Communicating directly means you don't make assumptions, you don't hint, you're not devious, and you don't go through other people in order to share your message. All these approaches lead to distortions. One of my favorite examples is of the woman who tried to get her point across to her husband by making sweeping generalizations about what "everyone" thought or felt. Her husband stayed out late quite often, and she felt irritated. But she didn't want to be direct about her emotions.

One day she said, "Some wives would be angry at your staying out so late at night."

"You mad or something?" he asked.

"Oh, no. *I'm* not," she said. "But *some* wives would be."

When you *are* direct, you speak the truth by stating your real needs and feelings. When you ask questions, you ask truthful ones.

How can a question be devious? Easily. If you ask a question and you want only one type of response, that becomes a setup. "Do I look fat in this dress?" or "I'm not looking any older, am I?" are questions you don't want to hear *or* answer. When you ask, your partner should have the freedom to give his or her own honest answer, no matter how you respond. *If you don't want to hear an answer, don't ask a question!*

If you feel angry about something, don't say you're tired. If you don't want to go to a social gathering, say so instead of "Oh, I don't know. I guess I could go for a while. . . ." By not being completely honest, we create false impressions, find that our needs aren't being met, and perhaps protect ourselves, but in the long run we create distance between ourselves and others.

When I'm confused about a person's message to me, I just ask, "What are you saying? I would like to be sure I understand you." This puts responsibility on the other person to clarify. Sometimes I have to repeat this two or three times to draw out the real intent. Creating an atmosphere of comfort that will assist the other person to share is one of the listener's important roles.

When you talk, ask yourself: *Why am I saying this? What do I want to say? What do I want the other to hear?*

Be Aware of the Importance of Timing

An old proverb states, "A word spoken at the right moment, how good it is!" (Prov. 15:23). Most emotions should be shared at the moment you experience them, since delaying distorts them. When you respond immediately, you allow your spouse to learn what you feel and need. For example, in a conversation, what's important to you may not seem significant to the other. Delaying your response may allow the person to totally forget what he or she said. Then he or she wonders what you're talking about when you bring it up later, and you end up wondering why he or she is so insensitive in not remembering.

We also need to give an immediate response to minimize *our own* distortion. Most of us aren't aware of how we distort messages, but we all do it sometimes. Why do we distort? *Because what we see and what we hear are often confused or affected by what we think and feel!* There's clutter in our minds. Filters are working.

That's right. The feelings we experience, as well as our immediate or previous thoughts, can distort what we take in through our eyes and ears. To avoid confusion, sometimes I ask myself, *What have I been thinking about Joyce? Are my thoughts valid at this time? What am I feeling right now?* By asking myself these questions while we're still communicating, I give myself the opportunity to clarify her point of view. Maybe I need to ask her a question or share what she did again. At the same time, I've learned to delay my own reaction long enough to help me understand the meaning Joyce wants to get across.

Are you aware of the two most critical times for communication between a husband and wife? These involve just four minutes. One is the first four minutes of the day that you see one another and the other is the first four minutes when you're reunited at the end of the day. These eight minutes can set the tone for the day as well as the evening. This is a time where you can share your love and interests and affirm one another, or this can be a time full of angry, griping, critical, attacking comments. What's shared sets the tone for the rest of the day.

Examine the patterns you've established in your marriage. Do you say the same things to each other morning after morning and evening after evening? Think about the way you've responded to each other each morning for the past week and compare your responses with the following:

Are you a *silent partner*? "Don't expect me to talk until I've had my third cup of coffee."

Are you a *commander*? "Okay, we have ten minutes to get into the kitchen. I want scrambled eggs, crisp bacon, and half a grapefruit. Come on, come on, get up. You take a shower first. I'll give you eight minutes. Then I'll shave. . . ."

Are you an *efficiency expert*? "You know, Joe, I tell you every morning, if you'd wake up at seven instead of seven-thirty, you'd have five minutes for your hot shave, seven minutes to shower, six minutes to shine your shoes, eight minutes to dress, and four minutes to comb your hair. Then you could come to the kitchen just as I'm putting the eggs on the table. Now, why don't you listen? I tell you this every morning."

What do you want in the morning? Closeness and intimacy or quiet and privacy? Have you ever shared with one another what works best for you? Some are morning people, some aren't.

The second important time of the day impacts what happens the rest of the evening. How you interact at this time can determine whether you spend the evening at the North Pole or on the warm sands of a Hawaiian beach. So, what happens between the two of you? Is it a time of factual reports about the news, the weather, the kids' misbehavior, or other bad news? Is it a time of silence and grunts?

Some spouses complain that the family dog gets more attention than they do. And it may be true. Dogs are talked to, caressed, patted; they get their ears rubbed and their backs and chins scratched. Not a bad way to greet your partner! Touching, asking feelings questions (see chapters 8 and 9), expressing delight in seeing the other person, should make the evening better.

Greet your spouse after a period of being separated (even if only for a few hours) with a smile, pleasant talk such as a happy greeting, touching and kissing, a compliment, humor, or recounting one of the day's interesting or "success" experiences.

If you need some space for a while when you arrive home, let your spouse know it, but let him or her know when you'll re-enter his or her life as well. It's worth the effort.

Set aside a period of transition between work—or any potentially stressful activity—and other parts of the day. This transition time is designed to provide a "decompression period" so that any pressures, frustrations, fatigue, anger, or anxiety that may have arisen will be less likely to affect marital communication. Some visualize how they are going to respond to each family member. Other couples take twenty minutes when they arrive home to sit in a dimly lighted room and listen to a favorite CD with very little talking.

Never discuss serious subjects or important matters that involve potential disagreement when you or your spouse are overly tired, emotionally upset, sick, injured, or in pain. Set aside a special agreed-upon time every day to take up issues involving decision making, family business, disagreements, and problems. Decision Time should allow for the relaxed and uninterrupted discussion of all decision-making and problem-solving activities. No other activities should be involved, such as eating, driving, or watching television. Take the phone off the hook. It may also help to set a time limit.

Jot down items as they arise. When you pose a problem or lodge a complaint, be specific as to what you want from the other person. Do you want anger, defensiveness, resistance, and continuation of the problem? Or openness, cooperation, and a change on the part of the other person? The way you approach the problem will determine your spouse's response.

Example: "You're not involved enough with the children."
Better to say: "I appreciate the time you spend with the chil-

dren and so do they. I know you have a lot going on, but we would all appreciate your evaluating your schedule so you could spend more time with them."

What static interferes with your communication? Is it your feelings, thoughts, physical state, or something else? Discover this and take corrective action, and your communication will improve.

Know Exactly What You Are Going to Say and Say It

When you talk with another person, do you want to share your *feelings, needs, thoughts,* or *observations*? Or do you share all four? Sometimes we blend and run these together so much that we lose all clarity.

When you share a thought, you offer another person your conclusions, your observations, your value judgments, or your beliefs and opinions. How do you state these? In such a way that your partner can understand, wants to continue listening, is interested? Do you ever indicate that what you are sharing is a thought rather than a feeling?

When you share an observation, you talk like a scientist, a police detective, or even a refrigerator repairman. There are no speculations or conclusions. You share the facts! "I have lived in Long Beach thirty-one years" is strictly factual observation. "I think I might end up living there another ten years, if plans continue as they are" is a thought based on some data I haven't yet shared with you.

Thoughts and conclusions are relatively easy to share. Feelings are more difficult. Why? Because our feelings may be a threat. The other person may not want to hear about my anger, grief, depression, sorrow, or elation. Many don't understand feelings, so from their point of view I'd be speaking a foreign language. In fact, some people in our society have been raised emotionally handicapped. They have no feeling awareness and no vocabulary for expressing feelings. But if you want deep intimacy to occur in a relationship, you *must* share your emotions. Yes, feelings statements are risky, but the potential rewards are worthwhile. Really it is quite easy to express them.

Verbally, you can describe your feelings four ways:

1. Identify or name the feeling: "I feel angry." "I feel sad." "I feel good about you."

2. Use similes and metaphors. We don't always have enough labels to describe our emotions, so we sometimes invent similes and metaphors to describe feelings. "I felt as if a cool breeze were blowing through the air." "I felt so bad, you'd think a herd of elephants had run over me during the night."

3. Report the time of response or the action your feelings urged you to do. "Right then I felt like hugging you." "I was so upset I felt like dumping my dinner plate in your lap that night."

4. Use figures of speech, such as "The sun is smiling on me today." "I felt as if a dark cloud were following me around yesterday."

How do you share your needs? Do you do it consciously? You alone can tell what you need and want and communicate that to others. In order for them to know, they must hear about it. Again, your partner isn't a mind reader. If you believe he or she is, get ready to be disappointed and angry! When you feel he or she should be, if you decide to share your need, it will probably come across as a demand, which the other person will resist. Instead, express your needs in a pleasant tone of voice, with clarity, and without blame or judgment. Needs are just simple requests of what would help or please you.

Whether you share a need, feeling, observation, or thought, people may wonder what your purpose is and what you intend. Let them know your *intentions*, and your communication will begin to bring results.

Wife: I want very much to end this argument.

Husband: I didn't know that. I thought you were too upset to stop. Sounds good to me—I'd like to come to some conclusion too.

Document what you say with facts, or if you are making an observation about another person, use some descriptive behavioral data.

• I think you're elated. I see a smile on your face, and your voice sounds up to me. Your tone of voice makes me feel you are upset over something. What's on your mind?

• I'm kind of concerned. You're frowning, and I'm not sure what that means. Don't you understand, or do you disagree? It would help me if you could tell me what your frown means.

• I wonder if you feel all right. You seem to be moving more slowly today. You look kind of down in the mouth, and your voice seems kind of flat. Do you think you could be catching the flu?

By knowing what you are going to say and saying it, you will avoid a communication booby trap! When you are not in tune with your own words, you tend to give partial messages. That's a booby trap because it creates a false impression for the listener. The authors of the book *Messages* talk about how important it is to stay in tune and send whole messages.

Whole messages include all four kinds of expressions: what you see, think, feel, and need. Intimate relationships thrive on whole messages. Your closest friends, your mate and your family can't know the real you unless you share all your experiences. That means not leaving things out, not covering up your anger, not squelching your wants. It means giving accurate feedback about what you observe, clearly stating your inferences and conclusions, saying how it makes you feel and if you need something or see possibilities for change, making straightforward requests or suggestions.

When you leave something out, it's called a partial message. Partial messages create confusion and mistrust. People sense something is missing, but they don't know what. They're turned off when they hear judgments untempered by your feelings and hopes. They resist hearing anger that doesn't include the story of your frustration or hurt. They are uncomfortable with demands growing from unexpressed feelings and assumptions.[1]

Of course in some situations you don't express all four, but your communication still works effectively. You don't share whole messages with everyone. Often as we talk with friends, some conversations are just informational. But if we leave out a significant part, we've only partially communicated.

Questions: When you share, are you sharing what is an actual fact based upon what you know from reading, hearing or observing?

Have you labeled and identified your conclusions?

Do you share your needs as requests and not demands?

Are you giving whole or partial messages?

You may be thinking, *Communication is a lot of work.* Yes and no! Yes, at first, until these principles become a normal pattern for you, but as your sensitivity develops, it becomes easier and easier.

COMMUNICATION BEYOND WORDS

So far I've talked about stating clearly what you want and intend to say at the proper time. Now I'd like to consider the elements that make up what I call your *paralanguage*. When you talk with your partner, you really don't depend upon words alone to make your point. You actually depend more upon the vocal component of your communication. It includes your pitch, the raising or lowering of your voice. It also includes resonance.

For four years I took trumpet lessons from an excellent young teacher. My teacher talked about resonance. He kept after me to "make the sound rich! Make it ring!" Now and then it did and I felt great when that happened. In speech, *resonance* refers to the richness or thinness of our voices. They can be thin and high or deep and full. With practice you can control both pitch and resonance.

Paralanguage also includes your articulation—how you enunciate your words. You can become so relaxed in your conversation that some of your words slur, or you may speak so precisely that each word sounds as if it's been bitten off and shot out of a gun.

The tempo or the speed of your words also forms part of your paralanguage. This factor reflects your attitudes and emotions. Remember a time when you heard someone talking fast? What message did he convey? Often it's excitement. Such people can be quite persuasive, but if their speech becomes *too* rapid we may start feeling a bit uneasy. In a normal conversation, talking too fast may be a sign of insecurity. On the other hand, a person who talks very slowly and deliberately may reflect either indifference or cultural upbringing. People raised in the country tend to talk more slowly than those from large cities.

Volume is another element in paralanguage. Loudness may reflect enthusiasm, confidence, or aggressiveness, or as in some speeches and sermons, it can indicate the speaker has a weak point in his presentation and wants to hide it by speaking more loudly. A soft voice can convey caring, understanding, empathy, intimacy, or a lack of confidence.

Finally, rhythm emphasizes certain words in a sentence. If I asked, "Are you going out tonight?" that's a simple question because all the words are alike. But note what happens when I change my emphasis: "Are *you* going out tonight?" or "Are *you* going out *tonight*?" If my secretary comes in late and apologizes and I say, "Oh, that's all right, it's only nine-thirty," my response seems reasonable and straightforward. But if I change just one word, I change the meaning and reveal much more about my emotions. "It's *only* nine-thirty" has a different message. If you say to me after I've made a request, "Wait just a minute," and give equal emphasis to every word, you make a request. But if the word *just* or *minute* is emphasized, you could be conveying irritation or annoyance.

I listen more for paralanguage than actual words, and I hope you do too. Why? Because through this people share their moods and attitudes. In this manner a person reveals more of what he feels than his words alone can communicate. As you watch a film or TV program, close your eyes and listen for the pitch, resonance, articulation, tempo, volume, and rhythm. The message is there. What does it say to you?

In the movies, robots' speech is monotonous. A few people talk in the same way. They don't vary their pitch, resonance, volume, tempo, or rhythm. When we hear them, we wonder, *Are they bored with life or themselves or what?* You see, your paralanguage often reflects your personality. It tells others who you are and even what you have to offer.

Over the past several years, I have suggested this exercise to hundreds of people: tape-record your family conversation around the dinner table for a week and then listen to the conversations. The value is tremendous. You not only have the opportunity to hear the interaction between family members, the words used, the interruptions, but you start to become conscious of your paralanguage.[2]

We don't often use just one element of paralanguage by itself but blend them to convey many varied meanings.

Is your voice reflecting what you want to say? Are your

words consistent with your voice? What do you like about your voice? What do you dislike?

Speak the other person's language. Be aware of what you want to say and how you sound. Remember that what you see and what you hear are often affected by what you think and feel inside.

Share whole messages to avoid communication booby traps.

Listen for your own and other people's paralanguage. Feelings and attitudes are shared in this manner.

ENERGY BUILDERS

1. What are your rules for clear communication? How have you already used them in your communication? What ones do you need to build skill in?
2. How can feelings complicate communication? When you communicate, do you share feelings, needs, thoughts, or observations? How does that influence the way you communicate? The way others understand you?
3. Have you given partial messages when you should have given whole ones? When? What happened? Have you received partial messages from others? What would have helped you understand them better?
4. What does it mean to have communication beyond words? What is paralanguage? Describe your own paralanguage. How do you enunciate your words? At what tempo do you speak? How loud is your normal speaking voice? How do you use pitch, resonance, and rhythm? Is it easy for you to vary these? Have others ever commented on them?
5. What will you do this week with the information in this chapter? Describe how your communication will be different.

3

What It's All About:
Speaking Another's Language
Step #3: Decipher Your Spouse's "Foreign" Dialect

O*ne Tuesday afternoon* I waited for my next clients, a young couple I'd never met who were coming in for their first session of premarital counseling. I looked forward to the challenge of working with them—I believe so strongly in the effectiveness and value of premarital preparation. As I walked through the waiting room, a new therapist on my staff stopped me and said, "Norm, I see you have a new couple coming in at two o'clock for premarital. I've never had the chance to conduct premarital yet, nor do I have much background in it from my schooling. What do you try to accomplish in the first session?"

At first I thought of sharing the eight topics I try to cover, but then I decided upon a different approach. "You know, John," I replied, "it doesn't really matter whether I'm seeing an individual, a married couple, or an engaged couple. In the first session, *among other things*, I try to learn *their* language and speak it. Once I do that, we're on our way. Well, here they are. I'll see you later."

As I turned to greet the couple and lead them into my office,

John stood there with a puzzled look on his face, mulling over what he had just heard.

ESTABLISHING COMMUNICATION

After the preliminary introductions, Jan, Bill, and I plunged into our topics. This young, alert, and eager couple wanted to build a marriage that would last and that would be fulfilling for both of them.

About halfway into the session, I paused, looked at them, and said, "I think it's about time to drop a time bomb on you, before we go any further." I paused, noticing that I definitely had their attention. They glanced at each other, then back at me. I continued, "I'd be remiss if I didn't share this with you early in our time together. The person seated across from you—the one you're about to marry—look at that individual right now, please." They turned and looked at each other with puzzled expressions.

"I just want you to remember," I continued, "that person is a foreigner. You're going to be marrying a foreigner!"

I paused and let my statements sink in. They looked at me, then back at each other. Jan raised her eyebrows as she faced Bill. Bill turned to me and asked, "What are you talking about, marrying a foreigner?"

I replied, "Just what I said."

Bill looked back at Jan and then at me. "What do you mean, 'marrying a foreigner'? We're both from this country." His voice took a staccato beat. "In fact, we couldn't be better matched or more alike! We were both born and raised in California; we're both white; our parents were born and raised in this country, and so were their parents. How are we foreigners?"

I laughed a bit and said, "Well, this comes as a shock to most couples, and I do share this with almost everyone I work with now. You and Jan *are* similar. But you were raised in different homes with different parents, siblings, experiences, and in effect, different cultures. You may eat the same types of foods, but they were prepared differently. You have different customs, different rituals, in your families, different beliefs and values, and you each learned a different language. If you want to have the kind of marriage you've described to me, your biggest task is going to be to learn about the other person's culture, to develop the flexibility to be comfortable with either set of customs, and above all, to learn your partner's language so that you can speak it!"

FALLING OUT OF TOUCH

Jan said softly, "You mean Bill and I, even though we've gone together for three years, still need to learn more about communication. You know . . . I *have* felt that way at times. On occasion I've sensed that Bill and I were sort of out of touch with each other, even though we had done a lot of talking and sharing. We'd talk and talk, and at the time we each seemed to grasp what the other person was sharing, but later I felt as if we hadn't talked at all. He didn't catch what I had said. Other times I have a difficult time understanding *him*. And I don't understand why."

"Jan," I said, "right now you're sensing and sharing something many individuals feel perplexed about for many years of their marriage. Bill, what do you think about this?"

Bill smiled slightly. "Yeah, I'm beginning to see what you're getting at now. Jan and I do talk quite a bit, but sometimes I wonder why she doesn't understand my perspective. I state my point of view, but from the questions she asks, it's as though she'd never heard me. So I try to explain again and again. In fact, at times I think we *over*talk about some things. I like to make everything clear and simple and to the point, but we tend to go on and—"

Jan interrupted, "Bill, the reason we go on and on at times is because you don't seem to get what *I'm* feeling. I need to make sure that I'm understood by you, so we don't have misunderstandings."

"Jan," I said, "it's important to you that Bill understands your feelings, right? Bill, you want Jan to understand your perspective and view it your way, right?" They both nodded. "Could it be that some of the words you use aren't in the other person's vocabulary? Could it be that in some way you're not speaking the other person's language?"

Jan replied first. "Perhaps that's what's happening." She thought for a minute and then continued softly, "Now that we're talking about this, I've become aware of something else. I feel we've made more progress, but at first we had to work on how we shared with each other. I didn't understand what was going on until I went to Bill's home for dinner the first time. What a shock!"

Bill laughed in instant recognition. "Yes, it was a shock for her."

"What happened?" I asked.

Jan replied, "We had dinner with his parents and two brothers and sister. Naturally, I felt a bit apprehensive, since I wanted to make a good impression. I felt a little on edge, and when I'm like that, I tend to quiet down. Not that I don't talk as much as I usually do, but I get more hesitant and soft-spoken. Once we got into dinner, I'm afraid I sat there with my mouth open in shock — at least I felt as if I did. Bill's family is totally different from mine. My family is polite, quiet, and they rarely raise their voices. If they do, *watch out!* It means someone is angry, but that doesn't happen often.

"But Bill and his family," she continued, "raise their voices, interrupt, carry on two or three conversations at once, even shout at times! I was numb by the time dinner was over and felt very uncomfortable. When we left, the first thing I said to Bill was, 'Bill, your family is such an angry group of people — and they don't seem very polite toward one another, either. They interrupted and didn't let people finish.' "

At this point Bill picked up the story and he was very animated. "That came as a big surprise to me. I asked her, 'What do you mean? My family loves each other! They're close-knit and loyal. In fact, they were just themselves tonight, which is good—real good! That means they liked you and looked at you as someone they could be themselves with. Nobody was angry. That's just the way we talk! We've always been that way, and so are my grandparents and aunts and uncles and their families! We're just loud and have our own style of communicating. I'm that way too.' "

"It was a shock for a while," Jan said. "The more I went with Bill, the more I discovered that he communicated that way. When he raised his voice, I froze. I thought he was angry, but I've learned he does that when he's excited and wants to emphasize something."

"So when you first went to Bill's home," I said quietly to Jan, "it was like entering another country, since they did things differently and, in a sense, spoke a different language. At first you felt a bit awkward, until you began to translate what they were saying into your own language. Am I right?"

They both laughed. "You're right," Bill replied. "Nobody ever put it that way before, but I can sure see how the idea of speaking another person's language makes sense."

FOREIGNERS UNITE

"This picture of marrying a foreigner is clearing up a bit for you then, isn't it?" I asked.

"Oh, yeah," Bill replied. "In fact, I can see how both of us have already started to learn each other's family language and to adapt to each family."

"How?"

"Well," Bill continued, "after some time I noticed that Jan started to open up when we were with my family. She actually raised her voice and even interrupted at times. She's learned to become one of us. I don't even think she was aware of the changes."

Jan spoke up. "Bill's right, I didn't think about how I was gradually changing, until one Christmas we had a tape recorder on during the family meal—or 'celebration,' as they call it. We sat and listened to it after dinner, and I was amazed when I heard myself. I sounded like them!"

"How did that feel to you, changing your way of communicating?"

"It was comfortable," Jan answered me. "I enjoyed myself and I was getting closer to Bill's family as well. I felt good about this new relationship with his family."

"Bill, did you adapt to Jan's family?"

"I sure did," he told me. "In fact, the first time I was with them I felt very uncomfortable. I didn't know if they liked me or not. They were so polite and soft-spoken. I notice now that when we're with Jan's family I'm comfortable, but I don't talk as loudly with them as with my own family. Her family doesn't talk all that much, but they have as much fun as my family. I've learned that's okay."

"Bill," I asked, "do you and your family understand one another when you talk? Do you grasp what each person is saying?"

"Oh, sure," he replied, "we make sense to each other."

Then I asked Jan, "Do you and your family understand each other when you share together? Are you in touch with each other?"

"Oh, yes," Jan said, "we always are. I get along especially well with Mom. Dad, I must admit, doesn't always say too much. I wish he would. He's short and to the point and gives *very* little detail. At times I feel we have to drag information out of him. When he does talk, he sounds like a newspaper reporter giving a condensed version of the daily news. He just gives the facts. I don't know when I've heard Dad share his feelings. That's frustrated Mom over the years too. But Mom and I really click."

UNDERSTANDING EACH OTHER

I turned the conversation back to the communication between this young couple. "Bill," I said, "you and your family seem to focus in well together as you talk, and Jan, you feel good about your communication with your mom. Now, what about the two of you together? What will it take for you two to communicate so that you understand each other?"

They looked at each other and then back at me. I waited and then said, "It's something to think about." I turned to Bill and, speeding up my rate of speech, asked, "By the way, Bill, are you and I communicating? Do you think we see eye to eye? Do we understand each other?"

Bill replied, "Oh, yes. You seem to see what I'm talking about. I'm getting the picture of this whole discussion of marrying a foreigner. I wonder, though, if I don't need a passport to marry Jan!"

We laughed, and I turned to Jan and asked softly, "How do you feel about our communication? Does it make sense?"

"Very much so," Jan answered. "You seem to have a handle on what I'm feeling, and what you say registers. We seem to speak the same language."

"Good," I said. "It's important that we learn not only to speak the same language but also to make sure we mean the same thing with our words. I've run into so many couples who get irritated and upset in their marriages because of such a simple matter as having different definitions for their words. You know, two people can speak Spanish and not mean the same thing. Two people can speak German and not mean the same thing. We're sitting here speaking English and using some of the same words, but we might have different meanings for them. Your experiences in life, your mind-set, what you intend can give meaning to your words.

"My wife might ask, 'Could we stop at the store for a minute on our way home, Norm? I'll just be a minute.' I might take the word 'minute' literally, but I'd better not. Years of experience have taught me we're talking about fifteen to twenty minutes."

Jan and Bill grinned and nodded.

"Bill, has Jan ever said to you, 'Could I talk to you for a minute about something?' and you said yes, assuming she meant a minute, but you're still discussing the issue thirty minutes later?"

They both looked amazed, and Bill spoke up quickly. "Tuesday night that very thing happened. Jan wondered why I was getting uptight."

Jan broke in, "Well, it was important. Did it matter how long it went on? You agreed we needed to talk about it, and I had felt that way for some time."

Bill responded, "Oh, no, it was all right. I just figured it'd be short, since you said a 'minute.'"

Jan replied with a bit more feeling, "But many times I feel *you have* set a time limit on our conversations. I almost sense that you're impatient and want to get to the bottom line. You don't want to hear all my reasons or feelings. In fact, I wish *you* would share more details with me. I wear a new outfit and ask you how it looks, and all you say is, 'It looks fine.' So, what's 'fine' mean anyway? You say 'fine' for everything! Can't you tell me any more about how you feel about it?"

Bill looked at me, rolled his eyes, then turned to Jan and said loudly, "But I said it looked fine. What else do you want to hear?"

I interrupted and said, "Bill, on a scale of zero to ten, with zero meaning it looks terrible—like it's out of the rag pile—and a ten meaning it's super—it's outstanding—where does the word 'fine' fall?"

Bill said, "Oh, it's somewhere between an eight and a ten."

Jan looked surprised and blurted out, "How would I know that? That's the first I've heard that 'fine' had any meaning at all!"

"This is what I mean," I interrupted, "when I say you need to define your words. Bill, if you couldn't use the word 'fine' and had to give a three-line description of the dress Jan is wearing, what would you say?"

Bill thought a few seconds and then said, "Well, I like it. The color looks good. The dress looks like you, and I like some of the detail around the waist. It fits well and I like the curves. It just seems to look like you. And the style is flashy."

I turned to Jan, "So, how do you feel about Bill's response?"

She smiled. "Now, that really feels good! He really seemed to notice, and I enjoyed hearing his description."

Bill jumped in and said, "Well, I could do that, but when I'm with some of my other friends and we say 'fine,' we know what we mean."

"I can understand that, Bill," I countered. "When you're with them you speak the same language, but when you're with Jan, you need to speak *her* language. She wants more detail, more description, more adjectives. That's what registers with her. Most men edit what they say to their wives. They think of details and decide, *Now, that's not important.* Anytime you think something isn't important, it probably is. This is a good example of what I mean by speaking the other person's language."

DETAILS: TOO MANY OR TOO FEW?

"Now that we're talking about it, which one of you tends to give more detail when you talk?" I looked back and forth between Bill and Jan and both of them pointed at Jan and laughed.

"I'm the detail person," Jan said. "Quite often Bill asks me to get to the point and give him the bottom line so he understands what I'm talking about. I just want to make sure that he's going to grasp what I'm sharing. I've always given a lot of detail and feelings, but sometimes it's as if he doesn't hear my feelings. He ignores them."

Bill replied, "I don't ignore what you're saying. I do see what you are getting at, but I don't always know what to do with those feelings. It's not that I always mind the detail, but I wish you would focus on the bottom line first, instead of going around the barn several times and then telling me what you're talking about. I like it straightforward and to the point."

I said, "Bill, you want Jan to communicate with you like a newspaper article."

"A newspaper article? How's that?" Bill asked.

"Most newspaper articles are structured like an inverted pyramid," I continued. "The first sentence is a complete summary statement of what is in the article. Next comes a brief paragraph with some of the most significant summary items expanded. The final larger portion of the article will contain the minute details."

"That's it!" Bill said. "An approach like that makes sense to me. I can follow what's going on a lot better, and"—he turned to Jan—"I'd be willing to hear some more of the detail. But I don't think I need to hear as much detail as you enjoy hearing. I don't want a two-line summary of what you say, but a *Reader's Digest* condensation would be helpful." They laughed.

"Bill," I said, "you're asking Jan to condense some of the details a bit and identify the bottom line right at the start. That helps you focus on her conversation better. Is that accurate?"

He nodded.

"That also means, Bill, since Jan enjoys detail, that when you share with her, you will give her more detail than you do now."

Bill nodded.

"Now, does my statement about marrying a foreigner make more sense to you?"

They both smiled and said, "Yes, definitely!"

"Once again let me go back to the question I asked a few minutes ago. Jan and Bill, what is it going to take, in addition to what we have already pointed out, for the two of you to understand each other and no longer be foreigners? What do you think, Bill? What do you feel, Jan?"

What do you as the reader feel? What are your thoughts about what needs to happen? What did you hear as you read through this account of Bill and Jan?

Now, before you read on, go back and read the interaction again. I did point out some steps for Jan and Bill to take, but I have not yet commented on a key principle. Read it again and listen to their conversation. See if you can grasp this principle. Which person did you respond to more easily or understand more clearly? Did one more than the other speak your language? What did I do as I interacted with Jan and Bill? What about my word selection?

ENERGY BUILDERS

1. Have you ever felt as if someone close to you were speaking a foreign language, even though you could understand all the words? Have you felt as if you were married to a foreigner? How have you been out of touch with each other? Why have you seen things differently? What did it take to hear each other clearly?
2. Have you ever had your words misunderstood by someone else because the two of you had slightly different meanings for the same word? How did it confuse your communication?
3. What kind of information do you want in a conversation? Do you like to hear the bottom line first, or do you want to hear all the details? How do you speak to others? Do you need to change your style when you talk to some people you see often?
4. What will you do this week with the information in this chapter? Describe how your communication will be different.

4

Learning Your Partner's Language
Step #4: Build on Your Common Ground

J an and Bill—a couple very similar to most in that their communication styles and patterns differ from each other—were on the
edge of a major breakthrough. As they continued their premarital
sessions they soon learned flexibility, which enabled them to speak
each other's language. This prompted them to begin thinking, *If
this is so effective in marital relationships, wouldn't it be effective in
work and social relationships as well?* They discovered a major
truth: speaking a person's language isn't limited to marriage or
courtship relationships. Actually I learned it by trial and error in
the counseling office over the years and decided if it worked so well
there, it would work in other places as well, and it does.

I'll never forget the couple who really introduced me to this
study of communication. Tony and Mary were a young Italian
couple whom I saw when I had my office in my home years ago.
To be honest, after the first two sessions of counseling, I was totally frustrated with them. I had gotten nowhere. I attempted to
be calm, rational, and polite, while they interrupted me as well as
each other. They shouted, attempted to outtalk each other and, as
far as I could see, followed no known rules of communication.

Learn the Other Person's
Rules of Communication

One Wednesday morning, I looked at my schedule and noticed that Tony and Mary were coming that afternoon. I thought, *Oh no. Here comes another experience in futility and frustration. They don't listen to a thing I say, and they don't seem to listen to each other either. Boy! Well, if you can't beat them, why not join them? Hmm . . . why not?* I decided to do just that.

When our session started, it soon evolved into two people talking loudly at once. I began talking loudly and they responded to me. It didn't bother them at all. Finally, I leaned forward, gestured to Tony to stop, and said quite loudly, "Tony! Tony! Listen to Mary. She's got something to say. Mary, go ahead and talk. Tony will listen."

Back and forth we went during the session. I felt like an orchestra conductor giving cues, raising or lowering the volume and pitch, controlling who was talking, and sometimes letting all three of us talk at once. I even shouted at them on occasion to get their attention! When the session ended, Tony didn't shake my hand. He pumped it, thanked me, and said, "Boy, was that a good session, Norm. See you next week."

I came out of the front room into the kitchen. My wife looked around the corner from the family room about fifty feet away and asked in a quiet voice, "Are you all right?"

I said, "Well, yes, why?"

"It sounded like World War III in there," she replied. "I thought people were going to start throwing things. Who was so angry?"

"No one was angry," I said. "We were just loud. That's the way they talk, and the only way they listen to me is if I become like them." From that point on we had some loud and wild sessions, and I enjoyed myself thoroughly! Instead of expecting them to adapt to my style, I adapted to theirs, and they became willing to listen to me and the suggestions I eventually made. Tony and Mary taught me and I'm indebted to them to this day.

Develop Rapport

We use the word *rapport* when we talk about establishing relationships with other people, and in the field of counseling, therapists are encouraged to establish rapport with the client as soon as possible. *Rapport* has been defined as "a relationship marked by harmony, conformity, accord or affinity."[1] It reflects a relationship that has agreement or even likeness or similarity.

No matter whom you meet in life, you will find that you have both differences with and similarities to that individual. But which do you emphasize? If you choose to emphasize your differences, you'll find it more difficult to establish rapport. If you emphasize what you have in common, you will be drawn closer more quickly. Look for your common ground.

People tend to like people who are like themselves. As one man put it, "Hey, it was great to go into that large group and discover several people who belonged to the same business club and read the same journals that I do. We hit it off right away, and I even have two invitations to dinner and racquetball!" We enjoy communicating with those who are like us, who have the same beliefs, values, hobbies, likes, and dislikes.

How do you choose your friends? Do you select those who are totally different from you, with not one area of common ground? Not usually. We choose our friends from a pool of people who help us feel comfortable with ourselves, and someone who is like us does that best. Perhaps this works as a subtle way of saying to ourselves that we're all right because there are others like us around.

How far does establishing rapport actually go? Do we have to become so much like others that we become clones? Not at all.

You'll still be who you are and reflect your own unique mannerisms and patterns of speech. However, by emphasizing similarities, you'll be able to respond to a much greater variety of people socially, in your business world, and in marriage. In order to establish rapport, you have to take the opportunity to learn to be flexible. In fact, I'd guess you already unconsciously do much of what I will suggest. Here I want only to identify it, refine it, and explain it for you so that you can become an even better communicator.

Mirror the Other Person's Behavior

Some of the outstanding therapists of our time are very adept at establishing rapport quickly. In watching them, you discover that part of their process of developing rapport relies on mirroring. *Mirroring* simply means giving back to the person portions of his or her own *nonverbal* behavior just as though the person were looking in a mirror.

We all do this to some degree. You go to a dinner party, and you find yourself matching your table manners and body postures to the expected level of informality or formality in different parts of the country. I think in advance which clothes would be appropriate. I don't want to overdress or underdress, compared to the group who will be there. I find that on the East Coast the dress is a bit more formal than in the Southwest.

Mirroring does not mean mimicking. From early childhood we have been taught that mimicking isn't acceptable. Again and again we have heard "Don't be a copycat," and we react negatively to such behavior. We have come to believe that mimicking is the same as making fun of a person, but actually mimicry is usually characterized by some exaggeration of a behavior or speech trait.

In contrast, mirroring occurs when you become sensitive to

portions of your own behavior and response and to the other individual. What do you begin to become aware of—portions of the other person's body posture, specific gestures, facial expressions, voice tone, tempo, and intonation patterns? In some cases I have seen the therapist match the person's breathing rhythms. But remember that these are very slight and subtle responses. If the person you talk with begins hitting himself on the side of the face every so often, don't do likewise. If the other individual comes running up after jogging four miles and is out of breath and panting, I wouldn't encourage you to mirror this behavior. Common sense has to prevail.

I'd suggest a *subtle* matching of slight behaviors, mannerisms, and voice. For this to be effective you don't have to be a therapist. Friends talking together, a teacher with a student, two business associates—anyone can do it. Unconsciously (and now more consciously) I have done it in conversations with people in social situations as well as in the counseling office. A slight shifting of the body in order to sit in a fashion similar to the other's person's, using a slight hand gesture that reflects one of his, pausing in the same way she does are all examples of mirroring. Be aware of what you do when you are with other people. Watch their interactions as they communicate. Notice the quality of the interaction when mirroring is there and when it isn't. It goes on all around us every day.

Let's go back to Jan and Bill, the couple to whom I gave premarital counseling. I asked if my statement about marrying a foreigner made sense to them, and they both said yes. Let's pick up the conversation where I left off.

"Once again let me go back to my question of a few minutes ago. Jan and Bill, what is it going to take, in addition to what we have already pointed out, for the two of you to understand each other and no longer be foreigners? What do you think, Bill? What do you feel, Jan?"

Bill thought a minute and then said, "Well, we need to speak the other person's language, right?"

"Right, but how do you do that, Bill? What does that mean in actual day-to-day communication?"

MIRROR THE OTHER PERSON'S LANGUAGE

Just then Jan spoke up, saying, "I might be off on this, but I'm beginning to catch a sense of what you've been doing with us."

"What's that?" I asked.

"I've noticed," Jan continued, "that, yeah, now that I think about it, you really have been doing this. You talk differently to Bill than you do to me. Now I know what you mean by speaking the other person's language. Bill, have you grasped it yet? No, let me take that back. Bill, do you see what Norm has been doing?"

With that switch in her vocabulary, I couldn't help but laugh. "You did it, Jan, you really do understand. You switched your vocabulary, which made sense to you, and used a word that's part of Bill's vocabulary. Bill, did you notice that?"

"Well, I noticed something different, but I'm not sure yet."

"Go on, Jan," I encouraged her.

"Bill," she said, "you use words like *see, look, focus* all the time, so they must have some significance to you. Those aren't my words, but I can learn to use them. When I use feelings words, I don't usually get much response from you, so perhaps I need to listen to your words more, and you need to listen to mine, and we can both learn to use each other's way of speaking."

Bill looked at Jan a minute and then slowly said, "Okay, I think I'm beginning to see—" He caught himself and then said, "You're right, I do use that word a lot."

"You know," Jan continued, "if we had a tape recording of this session—no, if we had a tape recording and a video recording, like the ones we used in our teacher-education courses—I imagine we would discover that Norm has been doing more than using our language. Norm, is that right?"

"Yes, it is," I replied. "You're perceptive to sense that so soon."

Jan smiled and said, "Now, if you had made that statement to Bill, how would you have said it?"

I laughed. "Bill, you're going to have to watch out for Jan. She really can see things quickly."

We all laughed at my choice of Bill's words, and Bill responded loudly, "I do see it now. You might say the same thing to each of us, but with different words, based on how we talk. I just noticed something else, Norm. When you talk to me, you give a bit more volume to what you say. Yeah, you do. You raise your voice just a bit, because I talk louder than Jan does. I noticed something else too. You don't waste any words with me on long explanations. You seem to make it short and to the point, and I like that. Maybe that's because that's the way I talk. This is really something. We haven't been here long, but it seems as if we've been together or known each other for a long time."

Jan broke in, saying, "Yes, I agree. I feel—and that's one of my comfortable words—the same way. I've noticed Norm does more than just speak our language with his choice of words. When he talks to you, he seems to shift in his chair and sits almost the way you do. It's nothing major, but he has done this several times. He sits up a bit more, which is the way you sit, Bill. When you talk to me, Norm, I've noticed you tend to sit back and put your hands on the arms of the chair, which is exactly what I do. You even slow down your rate of speaking and speak more softly to me than to Bill."

"You're right, Jan," I replied, "and I feel good about what you're sharing for several reasons. One is, I want to be sensitive to the people I talk with, whether it is in this office or outside the counseling environment. Second, I am not always consciously thinking of my choice of words or my body language. What you've just said lets me know that this way of responding to people is becoming more and more automatic for me. I'm delighted to see how quickly both of you are grasping this concept."

CONSCIOUSLY COMMUNICATE

"Since the two of you are just now becoming aware of this process," I continued, "it will take some work on your part to refine your communication with each other. I feel you've discovered the fact that you've probably responded this way already with other people. You just weren't aware of it. Now you'll become more aware and will work consciously on how you communicate, not only with each other, but in a wider range of contacts as well. What will each of you be doing differently in your communication with each other at this point? Bill, what do you think?"

Bill responded, "Well, since this is in my lap, let me think a minute." He paused a while, considering my question. "Boy, this is something. I feel as if—how do you like that, one of Jan's favorite words!—I've just come back from an archeological expedition and made a gigantic discovery, and I'm still trying to put together all the pieces I've unearthed!"

At this point, I broke in, "Bill, is that the way you usually describe things? Jan, was that a typical description for Bill?" They looked at each other, wondering who was supposed to answer. I looked from one to the other, saying noverbally, "Whoever wants to respond may."

Jan said, "I haven't heard descriptions like that too often, but it was great. It said so much more than 'I'm thinking about it,' or something to that effect."

"Well," Bill said, "it's just the way I was feeling, and that's the best way to describe it."

"Bill, that was great," I said. "That was a beautiful example of how to expand your description and give your conversation more life, meaning, and richness. As you begin to communicate more and more like that, you will be amazed at your own ability and other people's response to you. What you did we call *drawing a word picture*."

"Sometimes," Bill answered, "I even amaze myself! Well, here's what I'm going to be doing differently as I communicate with you, Jan. I guess the first step is to really learn your language, and that means I need to listen to you, to what you say, and how you say it. I'll have to listen to you with my eyes as well as my ears. I know there are times when I don't have eye contact with you when you talk; then when I do turn and look at you, your message somehow seems different.

"I don't think I'll totally change my way of communicating, since I want to be me. *But* when I talk with you, I can use some of your words and phrases. Would it help if I didn't talk as loudly or as fast?"

"Well," Jan replied, "I hadn't thought about it. Sometimes I do feel less on edge when you slow down and you're a bit quieter. But I don't want you not to be yourself, so let's play it by ear and see how I feel."

"Okay," Bill continued, "I could do that, I know. I know something that might help. What about my giving more detail when I share with you? Maybe I can expand my two lines into four, when I tell you a story or event." Bill grinned as he said it.

"Bill, that's an excellent idea," I commented. "You do give more detail than some men I've worked with. I've seen some who seem to reflect the old John Wayne, silent-cowboy image. They sit here and say, 'Yup,' and 'Nope,' and that's it. It's like pulling teeth to get any more out of them. You know what I did with one man? He'd had so much pressure put on him to talk more, and it hadn't worked, so I decided to take a totally opposite approach. I suggested to him that he *not* share any more than he had been and that he continue to respond with his typical words or 'Yup,' and 'Nope.' When he asked me questions, I began to respond to him with his same words. Did he look surprised! Once he saw what it was like, he began to open up and communicate, and we all discovered that he could share details.

"Bill, give more detail, and Jan will respond more. She'll also put less pressure on you to share, since you're already doing it. At times *I* have just given summary statements. Most men have this tendency. Now when I hear a friend or acquaintance who has a baby, instead of going home and telling Joyce the fact with none of the vital statistics, I write down the particulars, such as sex, name, weight, length, when born, and so on. Then I share that information, since that's what she wants to hear. I used to go home and say, 'So-and-so had a baby.' Joyce would ask, 'Oh, what was it? A boy or girl? When? How much did it weigh?' I would answer, 'Oh, I don't know. It was a kid. You know, a kid is a kid. That's all I know.' That doesn't go over too well at my house.

"Jan, when you share with Bill, condense a bit and give the topic and bottom line first, and you'll have his attention."

There was no question that rapport had been established during that initial session. We related very well together. Why? Because I took the initiative and learned their language. I didn't wait for them to learn mine or make them conform to me at the outset. Notice that they were very open to take my suggestions for new ways to communicate. Why did that occur so readily? Because of my pacing, a subject you'll find out more about in the next chapter.

Who are you most like, Jan or Bill? What is your style of communication? What will be your first step as you begin to incorporate these principles into your life in a new way?

Remember: speak the other person's language.

ENERGY BUILDERS

1. Have you ever known someone who had a communication style so different from yours that you found it hard to understand each other? What happened?

2. What does *rapport* mean to you? Do you have an easy time developing rapport with those who are like you? Why? How can you increase your rapport with those who are different from you?

3. What does *mirroring* mean? How is it different from mimicking? How can you mirror someone else's nonverbal messages? Verbal communication?

4. How can you refine your communication with others? Do you speak the same language? What will be three benefits of speaking the other person's language? Give an example of how you did this today.

5. What will you do this week with the information in this chapter? Describe how your communication will be different.

5

I Married an Alien — But from What Planet?

STEP #5: UNLEARN OLD HABITS THAT DON'T WORK

It was ten o'clock on a Wednesday morning. My first appointment was scheduled to arrive in just a minute and I looked at the names. It was a new couple—a pastor from the area had referred them. The call had come in the day before, and since I had a last minute opening, I was able to schedule them. But there had been no opportunity for them to complete the customary preliminary forms that would have given me a great deal of information. We would just have to find out the difficulties during their first session.

Herb and Sue, a well-dressed middle-aged couple, came in and sat down. After a few minutes of casual conversation, I asked, "What brought you to the place of wanting to see a counselor? What are your concerns?"

Herb looked at me, leaned forward, and said in a quiet, tense voice, "I want to know just one thing. I've been married to this woman for seventeen years of fighting. Hassle, hassle, hassle. That's all our marriage is—*one big hassle!* We can't agree on anything. We are so different. I'm not sure we should even be married. I don't have this problem with people at work—we get along great. Now *you're* the so-called expert. You tell me why there's so much conflict in our marriage. Do other people have this many problems?"

Sue looked up at that point to share her opinion. The next fifteen minutes seemed to escalate into a small-scale border war, and I felt I was right in the middle of it. They interrupted, raised their voices, made accusations, and threw critical barbs back and forth. Finally I raised my voice and said, "Thank you!"

They stopped and looked at me, then back at one another. "Thank you?" Jim said. "For what?"

"For answering your own questions of a few minutes ago. You asked why you have so many conflicts. That last fifteen minutes just exposed the answers. Would you like to know what I heard?"

They both looked at me and Sue said, "Yes, I would like to hear. We've been trying to figure it out for years. What did you discover?"

I said, "You asked for it, and here it is. I heard some of the most common issues that create problems for the majority of couples. I heard unresolved issues from your past, Sue, and you both have unfulfilled needs and expectations. You haven't accepted your personality differences and you are still trying to make the other person into a revised edition of yourself. You engage in some classic power struggles and you keep the conflicts alive by the intense, vicious circles you've built up. Finally, you've never learned to speak the other person's language. Now that's just for openers."

They looked at each other silently and then back at me, nodding in agreement. I continued: "You're looking for a marriage of peace, harmony, and fulfillment. You've spent seventeen years constructing negative patterns. That's the bad news. The good news is *you can change*. I don't mean change your personalities. Couples who make it in marriage are not carbon copies of each other. They are people who have learned to take their differences through the process of acceptance, understanding, and eventually complementation, and they learn to speak their partners' language. Differing from another person is natural, normal, and can add an edge of excitement to a relationship."

A SPOUSE FROM *Star Trek*

Differences. How do you learn to adjust to the differences in your partner without losing who you are? How do you learn to appreciate another person's uniqueness? How can you learn to live with this person who is so, so different from you? As one wife said, "It's just not that I married someone who's a foreigner. At times I feel like I married an alien from another planet! Did I join the cast of *Star Trek* or marry someone left over from the film series *Star Wars*? Help!"

I've heard them all: questions, complaints, pleas for help. For years people have asked me the question, "When you marry, do you end up marrying someone who is your opposite or someone who is similar?"

My answer is, "Yes." I'm not copping out by saying that. The answer *is* yes! It's both. There will be similarities as well as opposites, and you have to learn to adjust to both. Think of it like this:

> We marry for our similarities.
> We stay together for our differences.
> Similarities satiate, differences attract.
> Differences are rarely the cause of conflict in marriage.
> The problems arise from our similarities. Differences are the occasion, similarities are the cause.
> The differences may serve as the triggering event, as the issue for debate or the beef for our hassle, but it's the similarities that create the conflict between us.
> The very same differences that initially drew us to-

gether, later press us apart and still later may draw us near again. Differences first attract, then irritate, then frustrate, then illuminate and finally may unite us. Those traits that intrigue in courtship, amuse in early marriage, begin to chafe in time and infuriate in the conflicts of middle marriage; but maturation begins to change their meaning and the uniqueness of the other person becomes prized, even in the very differences that were primary irritants.[1]

Differences abound in any marriage. Generally, they can be divided into two types. The first includes those that can't be helped, such as age, race, looks, home, and cultural background. Your personal body metabolism will affect where you want the temperature in the home, whether you need an hour to get both eyes focusing. These differences cannot be changed.

But the other type of differences involves those that can be changed. These can include personal habits in the bathroom or at the dinner table, whether you like to get up early and your spouse enjoys sleeping in late, or whether one likes going out three nights a week and the other prefers watching television at home. I'm amazed at how small learned behaviors, such as having the bedcovers tucked in rather than having them loose or eating a TV dinner rather than a four-course dinner on a tablecloth, become such major issues in marriage.

STAYING FLEXIBLE IN OUR STRENGTHS

We're all different. We're mixtures of various tendencies and preferences. We've been talking about these throughout this book. And these are neither right nor wrong. The problem arises when one of these tendencies becomes so strong and dominant that our strengths become weaknesses. This condition fails to allow for alternate ways of responding to life. As a result, we become entrenched in our own styles and threatened by differences. Remember this: the person who has the greatest flexibility and who can respond to situations in a variety of ways will derive the most out of life and impact the greatest number of people.

What are some of these tendencies that draw us to each other but can end up being a pain in the neck? Well, some of us are thinkers and some are feelers. Some of us are savers and some are spenders. Some of us are amblers and some are scurriers. Some of us are inner people and some are outer people. Some of us are bottom-line and some are ramblers.

The factor of timing becomes an issue for many couples as they attempt to deal with marital adjustments. We all have different internal clocks. Some of us use a calendar to tell time, others a stopwatch. Often these two people marry each other. A wife needs ten minutes to get ready; her spouse chews each bite five times. One spouse tells a story in three minutes and the other takes ten to tell the same story.

PROBLEM-SOLVING STYLES

The way people approach problems and attempt to solve them can also become an issue in a marriage. Some individuals are leapers; others are lookers. Leapers do look, but it's usually back over their shoulders after they've made a decision. This has often been called the *intuitive approach*, whereby a solution just leaps into a person's mind. Rarely are the answers totally correct, but neither are they totally wrong. Leapers tend to rely upon past experiences to make their quick decisions.

Then we have the lookers. They are the calculators, the people who tend to do things by the book. They look at a problem, identify the elements in it, and then come up with a solution. And they often tell you that both their approach and their solution are right. And guess what: they *are* right most of the time! This really frustrates the leapers. But the lookers need all the available data for their decisions to be correct.

Both approaches have strengths and advantages. If you need a quick decision in an area that is not all that important, the leaper is the best one to decide. But when you have a problem that is quite important and you need all the facts, the looker is the best approach.

No couple are compatible when they marry. The challenge of marriage is to learn to become compatible. Some accomplish this within the first few years, some within ten to fifteen years, some . . . well, unfortunately some never do. I know: I've seen them in my counseling office, some at seminars, some informally. But the sad part is that it doesn't have to be that way

I don't care how different a husband and wife are, it's possible to learn to adjust, to adapt, to live in peace and harmony, to be compatible. I've seen it happen. One of the delights of counseling is to see couples both in premarital counseling and those who have been married for thirty years discover how to understand, accept, adjust to, and honor their partners' uniqueness.

Messages from the Trenches

I've worked with this issue for years. I've taught about it and written about it in several books. And yes, I'm going to write about it here, although in a different way. I'm going to let married individuals tell about their spouses and themselves and what they have learned. I won't give any guarantees, but I suspect that you are going to identify in some way with one or several of these people. Hopefully, you can learn from what they have learned.

These accounts are from those who have been married for a while. Some of them struggled through this process before the pieces came together.

Tom's Tale

My name is Tom. I'd like to tell you about my outgoing, social wife. That's what I call her now, and that's what I called her before we married. But after about two years of marriage I started calling her "Mouth"! She talked and talked. She even talked to herself. Now me, I'm just the opposite. I don't talk much at all. At first I was attracted to her mouth. Then I was repulsed by it. My ears get exhausted.

I couldn't understand why Jean had to think out loud so much. It's as if she wanted the whole world to know about her wild ideas. And it's not just because she's a woman. I've seen men who are the same way. But it seemed as though she'd start talking before she engaged her brain. At times I felt my space was invaded by her giving a running commentary on everything or saying the same things over and over or wanting an immediate response from me on a question I'd never had a chance to think about. Man, all that stuff wore me out.

There were even times when I'd go to the garage to putter around (and find some peace and quiet) and Jean would come out there, bring up a subject, ask my opinion, arrive at her own conclusion before I could think about it, thank me, and walk out. I'd just stand there shaking my head and wonder, *Why even ask me?*

When we go to an activity, it's as if she knows everyone there and wants to stay forever. It seems as though she will never run down or get enough socializing. I've seen men like that too. I always wondered how they did it. It drains me but seems to give her a shot of adrenaline.

Oh, and wait until you hear this: I think I'm a caring guy. I do give compliments. Maybe not as many as I could, but I don't think I could ever give enough to Jean. She is so capable and gifted. But it seems as though she doesn't believe it unless I or someone else tells her. I used to wonder why she would ask me how she did or how she looked when the answer was obvious: fantastic!

And something else bugged me—Jean is better about this now—she'd interrupt me when we talked. It takes me longer to get things out and reach a conclusion. So, if I talked or thought too slowly, I either got interrupted or she finished my statement for me. We had a good discussion (argument) over that one. But she's much better now, and I don't avoid discussions with her. Sometimes I remind her that our speeds of thinking and speaking are different and that helps.

When we have a conflict I think (or used to think) there was just too much talking about the problem. Jean had the belief that if we just talked it through a bit more, everything could get resolved. Resolved? A few more words would be the last straw. We eventually learned to put some time limits on each segment of the conversation so I could have time to think. Then I was ready to continue. I also worked on sharing my first reaction without having to do so much thinking and editing.

Now and then I've said to Jean, "Honey, I want to resolve this, but since I'm getting worn down, why don't you write out what you're thinking or put your thoughts on the computer? Then I can read them over and be able to respond. Okay?" That's worked well for us. That way Jean doesn't get as loud either, since I tend to withdraw when that happens. I used to tell her, "You're not going to get me to respond by shouting at me. It won't work." Now I say, "I want to hear you. I would appreciate it if you would say it softly and give me a chance to respond."

Sometimes I would ask her, "Why are you bringing that up again? We've already talked about it." Jean would say, "No, we haven't." And then we'd argue over whether we had or not. This went on for years until one day I heard her say, "Could it be that you rehearse conversations in your mind and then think we've already talked about it?" Bingo!—that's exactly what I do, and when she said it, I realized it. Fortunately, we've learned to laugh about it. Sometimes I catch myself and say, "Yeah, I did talk to you about it . . . in my head."

Sometimes I worry about what Jean says to others about us and our intimacy. You know, our lovemaking. She likes to talk about it when we're not even doing it, and sometimes during a romantic time she wants to talk. That's not me. I don't say much, but I've learned that this is what Jean enjoys. And it's getting more comfortable.

What has really helped me (and us) is to realize that there's nothing wrong with Jean the way she is. That's just her. It's the way she's wired. I guess it's the way God created her. She's okay. I'm okay. We're just different and we can learn to adjust.

I've learned to appreciate the fact that she's helped me be more sociable and involved with other people. It's become apparent that Jean needs more interaction and time with people than I do. Now I'm glad to provide it. It's all right for her to go places and gab, and I can stay home or get together with one of my male friends.

It's really helped me to understand that Jean needs to talk to figure things out. And it doesn't mean that she's going to do what she's thinking out loud. She's just thinking. I've learned not to assume.

We're not perfect, but we are much more accepting. We've learned to be creative in the ways we approach each other. And it is a lot more peaceful.

Jean's Journey

Well, I'll try to be brief (that's a joke!). I'm an outgoing, talkative person who for some strange reason was drawn to a quiet, reserved, thoughtful man. I knew we were different when we were dating but never realized just how much until we were married. It really hit me the evening I figured out that Tom seemed to be avoiding me. Even when I was talking to him, it seemed as if he couldn't wait until I quit talking. And his responses were shorter and shorter. It was as though he thought if he said less, I wouldn't have so much to respond to.

I guess it was true, because eventually I'd get fed up and socialize on the phone. I actually felt rejected and hurt because I wasn't getting enough talking out of Tom. I couldn't figure out why he was like that. At first I thought, *That's just the way men are.* But others I dated weren't always like that. I've known women who are like Tom. So I figured it's just the way he's wired and put together.

I just love getting together with others. I get energized by them. But it doesn't take long (at least it seems to me) for Tom to get worn out at a party and want to leave early. I've even seen him just sit off to one side by himself or go into another room for a while just to be alone. I used to think, *What is wrong with that man?* Then I began to discover that Tom needs some quiet times and space to get energy back. That's draining for me, but it perks him up.

He's friendly and communicates well, but he doesn't go out of his way to connect with people. I've got scads of friends. He's satisfied with just two. See, there's the difference—just two! That wouldn't be enough for me. I need more people to talk with. And I love interruptions. They're just great, but they really bother Tom. It's as if he needs to know ahead of time that he's going to be interrupted.

One of our biggest conflicts is, or was, in the area of communication. I like to get things resolved, and that means talking through every part of an issue. But the more we talked (or *I* talked), the more he seemed to retreat. So I figured I'd just keep after him and he was bound to open up. No such luck! He'd retreat, clam up, or say, "I don't know." I admit I want answers right now. I used to say, "Tom, tell me right now. You don't need time. For Pete's sake, tell me!" And then nothing. Silence. It's as if I just short-circuited his thinking ability. And later on I discovered I did!

Tom is more of what they call an *inner person*. Through some reading I discovered he's the kind of person who likes to think things through in the quiet of his mind without pressure—and then he's got a lot to say. Now when I need his feedback or a discussion, I just go to him and say, "Tom, here's something I'd like you to think about. Put it on the back burner where it can simmer for a while and when it's done, let's discuss it." He appreciates it, and we talk more. And lest you think he always uses a Crock-Pot to cook, he doesn't. Sometimes it's a microwave! After I did this for a while he said to me, "Thanks for recognizing and respecting my need to think things through in privacy." That felt good, because I like compliments.

I've had to learn he isn't comfortable thinking and talking fast out loud. That's my world, not his. A few times we got into a conflict and I pressured him so much he just let fly with an outburst that seemed extreme. I learned not to push. It's better to let him think first.

I've also learned to not interrupt Tom with every thought that pops into my head. I'm finally learning to edit and pick times when I can have his attention. I know my thinking out loud used to bother him, because he thought I meant every word of it. I just like to sort things out, and I don't care who knows it. So now I just warn him, "Tom, I'm just thinking out loud again. You can relax, because I'm not going to rearrange all the furniture in the house today."

You know, I used to think that Tom's quietness and withdrawal at times were a passive-aggressive way of getting back at me. But they weren't. I just didn't understand it. Twice this last month he actually did some thinking out loud with me, which was wonderful. I know it was difficult for Tom, but it was great to see him put forth that effort. I hate to admit it, I really do, but now I see some value in being alone and quiet too . . . sometimes . . . just a bit.

I've also learned that when I encourage him to be who he is, I receive more of what I need too. The other day I knew he was frazzled, but I wanted to talk. Usually, I would have forced the discussion or tried to, but I remembered a couple of passages from a book: "Don't talk so much. You keep putting your foot in your mouth. Be sensible and turn off the flow!"

So I said, "You look as though you need some recouping time. Why don't you go read or do whatever, and maybe we could talk a bit later." And we did talk—quite a bit. And I am learning to write him notes too.

Tom understands things that used to really get me. He's better at it, but I've learned that a few of his words mean a hundred of mine. When he gets a big smile on his face and doesn't say much, I say, "It looks as if that smile is about five hundred of my words." And he says, "You've got that right. I just love good translators!"

So I've learned to give him time and space and not to interrupt when he talks. And I don't assume anymore that he doesn't have opinions or want to talk. He's selective and more methodical. I use a scattershot approach.

In what way are you like Tom?
In what way are you like Jean?
In what way is your spouse like Tom?

GROWING THROUGH OUR DIFFERENCES

These two couples, as well as so many others, have gone through the typical stages of adjusting to conflict. You're vaguely aware of them when you marry. You certainly wouldn't say at that time that your partner is different—more likely "unique." But after a while he or she is . . . different.

At first you may try to *accommodate*. You tolerate, overlook, or you substitute unique for differences to avoid conflict.

Then you *eliminate*, or try to purge the differences in one another by demanding, pressuring, or manipulating.

But then you *appreciate*, because you discover the differences are necessary and indispensable. They're essential.

And because of this you are able to *celebrate* them. You delight in them. You welcome them. You encourage their growth.[2]

Couples discover through this process that they didn't marry the wrong person. Think about this:

> In reality, we marry the right person—far more right than we can know. In a mysterious, intuitive, perhaps instinctive fashion we are drawn by both similarities and differences, by needs and anxieties, by dreams and fears to choose our complement, our reflection in another.
>
> We always marry the right person, and the discovery of that rightness moves us into the third marriage within a marriage. We at last begin to appreciate what we had sought to eliminate.
>
> As we discover that we knew more than we knew when we chose whom we chose, appreciation begins to break into a gentle flame. In appreciation, we discover that people who marry each other reflect each other. There is a similar level of maturity, a parallel set of self-understandings and self-acceptance in most couples choosing each other. The two express their self-image and self-valuation in the person selected.
>
> People who marry each other complete each other in a puzzling yet pronounced way. The missing is supplied, the imbalanced is brought into equilibrium, the dormant is enriched by what is dominant in the other.[3]

Well, what do you do now? Study your partner. Study yourself. Decide how you could respond differently. Expand your knowledge of gender differences, personality differences, and how to speak in a language that your partner understands. We've just scratched the surface here.

You may be surprised and amazed by what you discover. And you know what? It will be worth the minimal amount of time it will take to bring a new and better level of harmony and adjustment to your marriage. It's an ingredient for a lasting marriage. It will help you celebrate your differences.

The adventure of marriage is discovering who your partner really is. The excitement is finding out who your partner will become.

ENERGY BUILDERS

1. List five ways in which you and your spouse are different and five ways in which you are similar.
2. Describe how you and your spouse complement each other.
3. Describe your problem-solving style and your spouse's. What are the strengths of each?
4. Describe how you have grown through your differences.

6

Who's Listening?
STEP #6: LEARN TO LISTEN TO MORE THAN WORDS

L isten? *Who's listening?*" That's a good question. Wherever you go, you hear a lot of talking. But real listening? That happens rarely, especially since so many have their own agendas. But if there's no listening, there's not only no communication, there's no relationship. There's no getting along. And you can't learn the language unless you listen.

One of the greatest gifts you can give to your spouse is the gift of listening. It can be an act of connection and caring. Often when two people are talking, their conversations are dialogues of the deaf. They're talking *at* one another. If you listen to your spouse, he or she feels *I must be worth hearing.* If you ignore your spouse, the thought could be *What I said wasn't important* or *He doesn't care about me!*

Have you had the experience of being really listened to? Not just heard, but *really* listened to?

Who would you say really listens to you in your family?

Whom do you really listen to?

Who's the best listener you know in your life?

Erik Weihenmayer may be the world's greatest listener. On May 25, 2001, he reached the peak of Mount Everest, surely a rare and remarkable feat for anyone. But Erik is completely blind. Suffering from a degenerative eye disease, Erik lost his sight when he was thirteen. But that didn't stop him. On a mountain where 90 percent of climbers never make it to the top—and 165 have died trying since 1953—Erik succeeded by listening. Listening very well.

Erik listened to the bell tied to the back of the climber in front of him so he would know which direction to go. He listened to the voice of teammates who would shout back to him, "Death fall two feet to your right!" so he would know what direction not to go. He listened to the sound of his pick jabbing the ice so he would know whether the ice was safe to cross. To say that Erik Weihenmayer listened as if his life depended on it is no exaggeration.

Few of us will need to depend on our listening abilities as much as Erik, but we can all learn a great lesson from his feat.[1]

LISTENING DEFINED

What do we mean by *listening*? What do we mean by *hearing*? Is there a difference? We hear basically to gain content or information for our own purposes. Listening cares. Listening is being empathic. *Hearing* means you're concerned about what is going on inside *you* during the conversation. *Listening* means you're trying to understand someone else's feelings. Hearing is passive. Listening is active.

Let me give you a threefold definition of listening. Listening occurs when your partner is talking to you and:

1. You're not thinking about what you are going to say when he/she stops talking. You're not busy formulating your response. You're concentrating on what your spouse is saying and absorbing it. Too many are not listening to what's being said to them but are already listening to what *they're* going to say. And far too often we think we know what our spouses are going to say, so we put our minds on hold and tune them out. This isn't just not listening, it's discounting. We need to listen to one another as if we were listening to our spouse for the very first time.

2. You are completely accepting what your spouse is saying without judging what he/she is saying or how he/she says it. You may fail to hear the message if you are thinking that you don't like someone's tone of voice or the words he or she is using. You may react on the spot to the tone and content and miss the meaning. Perhaps the person didn't articulate the comment in the best way, but why not listen and then come back later when both of you are calm, and then discuss the wording and tone of voice? Acceptance doesn't mean you have to agree with the content of what's said. It means that you understand that what the person is saying is something he or she feels.

3. You can repeat what your spouse said and what you think he/she was feeling while speaking to you. Real listening implies an obvious interest in his or her feelings and opinions and an attempt to understand your spouse from his or her perspective.

Listening is sharp attention to what is going on. Listening to your partner means letting go of your concerns, wants, and investments in your own position long enough to consider his or hers. When you're doing the talking, you're usually not learning. When you're listening, you are.

You can learn to listen. Any husband or wife can. You can teach your mind and ears to hear more clearly. It's true. You can teach your eyes to see what they don't see now. But the reverse is also true. You can learn to *hear* with your *eyes* and *see* with your *ears*. You'd be amazed at what's being said that no one is hearing.

To Pay Heed

The word *hear* doesn't always refer to an auditory experience. It usually means *to pay heed*. As you listen to those around you, you need to pay heed to what is being shared. It means tuning into the right frequency. If you're struggling to communicate with one another, use the "radio approach" or RA. When you hear static on the radio, you *don't* adjust the volume control, you adjust the tuning knob. The more attention you pay to tuning, the better you hear. So, tune in to your spouse. It works the same.

Because my retarded son, Matthew, didn't have a vocabulary, I learned to listen to him with my eyes. I had no other option. He would grab our hands and place them on his head or rub his head against us to show us something was wrong. We learned to read his body movements and his eyes to detect any seizure activity. I could read his nonverbal signals, which carried a message.

Because of Matthew I learned to listen to what my counselees could not put into words. I learned to listen to the message behind the message—the hurt, the ache, the frustration, the loss of hope, the fear of rejection, the joy, the delight, the promise of change. I reflect upon what I see on a counselee's face, his posture, walk, and pace, and tell him what I see. This gives him an opportunity to explain further what he is thinking and feeling. He *knows* I'm tuned in to him.

Were you aware that every message has three components: (1) the content, (2) the tone of voice, and (3) the nonverbal communication? It's possible to express many different messages using the same word, statement, or question simply by changing our tone of voice or body movement. Nonverbal communication includes facial expression, body posture, and actions.

The three parts of your communication must be complementary in order for you to transmit a simple message. It has been suggested that successful communication consists of 7 percent content, 38 percent tone of voice, 55 percent nonverbal communication.

We're usually aware of our content, but not nearly as aware of our tone of voice. *You* have the capability of giving one sentence a dozen different meanings, just by changing your tone. Tape-record some of your dinner conversations sometime and then sit down and listen to yourself. Tape some conversations between you and your partner and then have a playback time. You'll be amazed!

I hate to admit it, but when it comes to tone of voice or variation of tone, men use more monotonous tones than women. Men don't open their jaws as wide as women, so they tend to sound more nasal. And men use only three vocal tones, whereas women use more than five. So men tend to use more choppy, staccato tones that can come across as abrupt and perhaps less approachable, at least to a woman. Women tend to have more flowing tones. And a woman will tend to use vocal inflections to emphasize a point, whereas a man uses loudness.[2] Sound familiar?

There's an old saying amongst speakers: when a point in your presentation is weak, raise your voice. I've heard hundreds of different speakers over the past forty-five years. Some were loud, some weren't. The loud ones (yellers or shouters) didn't have much impact on me. But those who made their points by changing tone of voice and pausing I really heard. Listen to others' tone of voice. Listen to your own. Listen to how some speakers use tone of voice.

In raising and training both shelties and golden retrievers, I've found that it's tone of voice that makes the difference. The right tone can cause them to come running to me, stop, or stay in place for several minutes. It's not loudness that makes a difference—it's tone.

How do you end your phone conversations? You don't come out and say you need to "terminate the conversation" or that you're "finished," do you? You use the change in tonal quality to accomplish this. One of my shelties taught this to me years ago. Prince had this unique ability to figure out when I was concluding a phone conversation. He'd show up during the last ten seconds of the conversation with a tennis ball in his mouth. It was as though he were saying, "I know you're about through. It's time to play ball."

I thought, *What's this? A psychic dog?* No. He'd figured out the change in my voice and put two and two together. (I just hate it when the dog is smarter than I am!)

WHEN NONVERBALS COLLIDE WITH WORDS

We often send confusing messages because the three parts contradict each other. I've done it. So have you. When a husband says with the proper tone of voice, "I really love you," but his head is buried in the paper on his desk, what's his wife to believe? When your spouse asks, "How was your day?" in a flat tone while passing you on the way to the other room, what do you respond to, the verbal or nonverbal message? What if you said, "It was lousy. I was depressed and threw up twice"? Would your spouse say "Fine" and keep on walking? If so, there's no real listening here.

You communicate nonverbally in two different ways. One is with body movements, such as gestures, your posture, and your facial expression. Our gestures send the listener messages. Some people talk with their hands a great deal. I happen to be one of those, and my daughter often tells me that if you were to tie my hands behind me, I wouldn't be able to talk. I don't think it would be that bad, but I do find myself gesturing even when I'm talking on the telephone.

We scratch our heads when we're puzzled or touch our noses when we're in doubt. When we want to interrupt we often tug one ear. A frustrated or angry person usually rubs his neck. We wring our hands to convey grief. We also rub them in anticipation.

What do you say with your face? What do others say with their faces? Turn off the sound of the TV some evening and concentrate on the facial expressions of the performers. In fact, if you have a VCR, record the program at the same time and watch it again later, with sound, to see if your perception was accurate. Browse through some magazines and as you do so, cover the people's bodies and just look at their faces. What do their facial expressions say to you? What do they intend to say with their faces? The more of the face you cover, the more difficult you'll find it to read emotions and attitudes. Our faces are the most expressive parts of our bodies.

The second way in which nonverbals communicate is in spatial relationship. How much distance you put between yourself and others conveys a definite message.

Were you aware that we communicate by the distance we stand or sit from another person? You've probably experienced the situation when you have had an argument with a family member and that person moved and stayed as far away from you as possible. Or a young couple in love have a heated disagreement, and she moves to the other side of the couch instead of sitting on his lap. These distances are obvious.

There are different zones people use when they interact with others. We use these unconsciously. Most of us don't think, *I need to stand two-and-one-half feet from this person, one-and-one-half feet from this one, and eight feet from that individual*—we just do what feels comfortable.

Intimate distance is quite close, usually six to eighteen inches from the other person's body. This is the distance used by close friends, those in love, and children hanging onto their friends or parents. Those who aren't intimate usually feel uncomfortable being this close to another person. Imagine yourself getting into a crowded elevator. Everyone there remains conscious of not touching one another. They pull their arms close to their bodies. Do they engage others in eye contact? Not usually. They avoid it. You have to stand at an intimate distance to get where you are going, but as soon as a few people leave the elevator, those remaining spread out.

To shake people up, get into a crowded elevator sometime and don't turn around. Stand facing the others, engaging some of them in eye contact! You'll make them uncomfortable unless you relieve their anxiety with a statement like, "You've wondered why I've called you here today" or "Is this the line to the men's room?"

Personal distance runs from one-and-one-half to two-and-one-half feet and is a comfortable distance for conversation. You can talk to friends or strangers at this distance at a social function and feel at ease.

Years ago at the graduate school where I teach, I had a student who was raised in Chile. His parents were missionaries, and for most of his life he lived there. My first encounter with him felt uncomfortable, since he stood very close to me. I mean just inches. It felt as if his face were right in mine. Unconsciously I began to put some distance between us by backing up a bit, but he moved closer. Finally he realized what was happening and shared with me that people in Chile have different distances than we do here. There the custom is to talk with another at an extremely close distance. (This gave new meaning to the phrase "In your face.") He also explained that he found most North Americans couldn't handle this, because of our training and culture. This is why many Latinos feel Americans are standoffish, and some Americans feel that Latinos are aggressive and pushy.

After my student informed me, I no longer backed off when

we talked together. I understood that his personal zone was much closer, so I accepted his distance and became comfortable with it. He left school and went on to join a church staff. Several years later I saw him and, remembering his background, I went up, said hello, and started to converse with him. I purposely stood very close, face-to-face, and noticed he started to inch back a bit. Then he caught himself, and we both laughed. He had become "Americanized," and I'd threatened him with my South American approach. Now both of us could shift either way, which gave us greater flexibility and comfort in talking.

THE POWERS OF NONVERBALS

Nonverbal expression serves several functions. It's a way of communicating attitudes. You'll see this everywhere. This can include how much you like the other or what he or she is saying.

If you're engaged in listening to someone, don't answer the phone. Don't let yourself be interrupted. One of the worst (and rudest) interrupters is the "call waiting" system on phones. If you're talking with your spouse and you hear the click, don't say, "Hold on a minute. I'll see who it is." How will your partner feel at that time? Not very important. When a clicking sound takes precedence over a couple's conversation, something is wrong. If you have call waiting, let *the other party* wait or leave a message.

When you're talking, don't let your eyes wander. If you don't have eye contact, you miss out. Remember this fact: *many people tend to repeat what they've said when they don't have eye contact with you since they're not sure you have heard them.* Sound familiar? Husbands complain, "My wife always repeats. I heard her the first time!" Wives complain, "His eyes were all over the place. He can't do two things at one time. How do I know he heard me?"

Your nonverbals reveal the emotion behind your words. One

of the best ways to elaborate and exaggerate a point you need to make is through your nonverbals.

Nonverbals are used as a ritual for saying hello, good-bye, and congratulations. You can use your nonverbals, such as a tender touch, when words are inadequate. What do you say to your partner with your nonverbals?

Every now and then I run into a married couple who make an appointment for counseling and begin the session by saying, "Our problem is that we don't communicate!" What they don't realize is that you cannot "not communicate" with others. You share your feelings and attitudes without saying a word. A person may lie verbally, but it is very difficult to tell a lie nonverbally. If you say you're happy or nothing is wrong and you look downcast, what should we believe—what you say verbally or nonverbally?

Too often the potential for sensitive listening and hearing lies untapped within us like a load of unmined gold. All of us have barriers that inhibit our listening. Some are simple and others complex.

Did you know that when you listen you have more influence than when you're talking? Are you aware *a listener* controls the conversation, not the speaker? Probably not. Most of us operate under the myth that the more we talk, the more we influence the other. What happens if both of you believe this? Your talking escalates and becomes more intense, but the words fly through the air with nowhere to land. Deafness prevails.

I've had some argue about the idea of a listener's controlling the conversation. Compare the listener to the driver of a car. The one talking is the engine. The engine provides the power, but the person at the wheel has the power to decide where the car will go. You, the listener, can give direction and guide the flow of the conversation by the statements you make and by the questions you ask. The more information you receive, the more you have to work with, and this happens by listening.

WHY SHOULD WE LISTEN?

Remember our threefold definition?

If you're a good listener, you should be able to repeat what your spouse said and what you think he/she was feeling while speaking to you. Real listening implies an obvious interest in his or her feelings and opinions and an attempt to understand the person from his/her perspective. When you listen, don't just listen to the words. Listen to the emotion, the feelings behind the words. This involves listening with your heart. And allow your spouse's emotions to touch you, and repeat what you've heard to make sure it's accurate.

This last statement is what is called *paraphrasing*. It reinforces the person talking so that he or she will continue to talk. When you verbally agree with the talker, you encourage him or her to share even more.

Did you know that healing of the cardiovascular system takes place when you listen to another person? Studies showed that blood pressure rises when people speak but lowers when they listen.[3]

One other thought about the listener. Some say, "When I listen, it seems to cause my spouse to just talk and talk and talk. Why?" Well, maybe it does initially, but if you remain perfectly silent, you'll create such tension within the person speaking that he or she will begin to back off. By not responding, you let the other know that you're through with your part of the conversation. (I'm not advocating use of the silent treatment. That's an unfair weapon that in time will erode a relationship.)

So, why listen? Why *do* you listen to other people? True, we've been taught and told to listen.

We listen to other people, especially our spouses to understand them, to enjoy them, to learn something from them, and to give help or comfort them.

OBSTACLES TO LISTENING

In order for caring listening to occur, we need to be aware of some of the common obstacles to listening. These exist especially in marriages.

Defensiveness

This is common. We're busy thinking up a rebuttal, an excuse, or an exception to what our spouses are saying. Do this and you miss the message, and there's a variety of good defensive responses.

Perhaps we reach a premature conclusion: "All right, I know just what you're going to say. We've been through this before and it's the same old thing."

Or we may read into their words our own expectations. We might even project onto them what we would say in the same situation.

Two other defensive indicators may be rehearsing our responses and responding to explosive words.

Explosive words hook you into a negative defensive response. They create an inner explosion of emotions. Explosives include "That's crude"; "That's just like a woman [or man]"; "You're *always* late"; "You *never* ask me what I think"; "I've been working harder than you!"; "You're becoming just like your mother." Not only do we react to explosive words, but we may purposely choose to use some that make it difficult for another to listen. What explosive words set you off? Which ones set off your spouse?

Not all defensiveness is expressed. Outwardly we could be agreeing but inside we're saying just the opposite. If your spouse confronts you about a behavior or attitude, do you accept the criticism or defend yourself? How would your spouse answer this question?

Interrupting

Another obstacle that hurts the listening process is similar to defensiveness—it's interrupting. You may erect this barrier because you feel your partner isn't getting to the point fast enough. Or you may be thinking ahead and start asking for information that would be forthcoming anyway. Your mind wanders and races ahead. You say, "Hold it. I've got a dozen ideas cooking because of what you said. Let me tell you some of them."

It is easy for our minds to wander, for we think at five times the rate we can speak. If a person speaks at one hundred words a minute and you listen at five hundred, do you put your mind on hold or daydream the rest of the time? We process information faster than it can be verbalized, so we can choose to stay in pace with the speaker or let our minds wander.

Sometimes men and women feel interrupted by the other because of the differences in what they're trying to accomplish with what they're saying. And remember, not all interrupting is interrupting. Some cultural groups don't use many pauses between turns in their conversation. Overlapping is just part of their conversational culture. Silence is seen as a sign of a lack of rapport. So overlapping is a way to keep conversation going. Some people use pauses. Others don't. Some are slow-paced and some are fast. Where you're from in this country will affect the way you speak in many ways. Many from California expect shorter pauses than those from the Midwest or New England. So when there's a conversation between them those from California appear to the others that they're interrupting. But someone from New York may appear to a Californian as interrupting.[4]

Personal Bias

Our own personal biases affect how well we listen more than we realize. For example, it may be easier for us to listen to an angry person than a sarcastic person; or some tones or phrases are enjoyable to listen to, whereas others are annoying; repetitive phrases someone uses (and may be unaware of) can bother us; excessive gestures such as talking with the hands or waving arms can be a distraction. Anything come to mind as you read this description?

Some are distracted in their listening because of the sex of the person who is speaking. Our expectations of what a man or woman shares and doesn't share will influence us. That's just great for marriage!

One hears with optimism and another with pessimism. I hear the bad news and you hear the good news. If your spouse shares a frustration, you may not hear because you don't like complaining; it bothers you.

Gender Differences

Lack of understanding of gender differences in listening and conversations create problems. Women use more verbal responses to encourage responses from the ones they're talking to. They're more likely than men to use listening signals such as "Mm-hmmm" and "Yeah" to indicate they're listening. But a man will use this response only when he's agreeing with what a woman is saying. You can see what the outcome of this will be. A man interprets a woman's listening responses as signs that she agrees with him. Meanwhile he's thinking, *That's good. We can move ahead on that new project.* But later on, he may become irritated when he discovers she wasn't agreeing with him at all. He doesn't realize she was simply indicating her interest in what he was saying and keeping the interchange going.

On the other hand, a woman may feel ignored and disappointed because her husband doesn't make these listening responses. And then she interprets his quietness as *He doesn't care*, or *He's not listening. He's just tolerating me!*

A man is more likely to make comments throughout the conversation instead of waiting for his wife to finish talking. And women seem to be more bothered after they've been interrupted or have failed to receive any listening feedback. That's why many women complain, "My husband always interrupts me" or "He never listens to me. He always has something to say." Women also use the pronouns "you" and "we" much more. This helps, since these words promote a sense of unity.

And keep in mind the following tendencies about a man's communication style. First, a man is more likely to interrupt the other person, whether male or female. Second, he is less likely to respond to the comments of the other person and frequently makes no response at all, tends to give a delayed response at the end of the other person's statement, or shows a minimum degree of enthusiasm. Anyone you know?

And last, a man tends to make more statements of fact or opinion than do women.

With all of these differences given the contrast between listening and talking styles between a man and woman, it's easy to see why misunderstandings arise. A wife might perceive her husband as uninterested or unresponsive. That may not be the case. It's just his way of responding to everyone, not just her. If a wife says, "He never listens to me" or "He disagrees with everything I say," it's more a reflection of his communication style than insensitivity.

Knowing about and accepting these differences can help you accept your spouse's style without being offended. This is one of the first steps of what we call *genderflex*—understanding the difference and making it a point to adapt and even use the other gender's style in order to bridge the differences.[5]

Personal Problems

Our own personal struggles may block our listening. We have difficulty listening when our emotional involvement reaches the point where we're unable to separate ourselves from the other person. You may find it easier to listen to the problems of others outside the home than to your own spouse. Your hearing is hindered by your emotional involvement, and listening may also be difficult if you blame yourself for the other person's difficulties.

Hearing what someone else is saying may bring to the surface feelings about similar problems we are facing. Our listening may be hindered if we're afraid that our emotions may be activated too much. A man may feel very ill at ease as his emotions begin to surge to the surface. Can you think of a time when, listening to another person, you felt so overwhelmed with feelings that you were unable to hear?

If someone has certain expectations for you, you may struggle listening to that person. If you dislike the other, you probably won't listen to him very well. When others speak too loudly or softly, you may struggle to keep listening.

Overload

You may find yourself facing yet another obstacle—overload. Perhaps you have used up all the space available in your mind for information. Someone else comes along with a new piece of information and you feel you just can't handle it. "I'm being bombarded from all sides and I don't have enough time to digest it all. Slow down." So it's hard to listen to anything. Your mind is like a juggler with too many items to juggle.

Timing

This is another common obstacle. Have you ever heard of comments such as these: "Talk? Now? At 8:30 in the morning? Give me a break." "Just a minute. There's only one more page to read." "I'd like to listen, but I'm already late for an appointment."

Did you realize there are times when listening isn't appropriate? It's true. And it's all right to let your spouse know you can't. It's all right to postpone listening to someone when you've already listened to someone else, you're under pressure for an immediate deadline, or you have to put out a brushfire—a crisis.

But you don't postpone by ignoring. Look at the person. Let

your spouse know you want to hear what he or she has to say and when you'll be available. Continue what you were doing, but make sure you follow through with your commitment.

Physical Exhaustion

Fatigue presents another obstacle. Both mental and physical fatigue make listening difficult. There are times when you need to let your partner know that this is not a good time. But tell him/her when you *will* be able to listen. (If you overuse this, you'll be in deep trouble.)

Selective Attention

You have a negative attitude that may ignore, distort, or reject positive messages. Often we hear what we want to hear or what fits in with our mind-set. If we engage in selective listening, we probably engage in selective retention. It's true you'll remember certain comments and situations and forget those you reject.

Go back over the obstacles to listening that I listed. Which will you work on this week? How can you become a better listener?

Do you know what the hindrances are to *your* listening? Who's responsible for the obstacle?

You *can* overcome the obstacles. The initial step is identify the obstacle. Of those listed, which obstacle do you identify as yours? Who controls this barrier—you or the one speaking? Perhaps you can rearrange the situation or conditions so listening would be easier. Have you ever thought of discussing this with your spouse? You may want to talk about what each of you can do to become a better listener and to make it easier for others to listen to you.

The Pause Button

Listen with your ears, your eyes, and your body. If someone asks, "Are you listening to me?" and you say, "Yes" while walking away or fixating on the TV, perhaps you aren't really listening. Concentrate on your spouse and the message. Give your undivided attention. Turn off the computer or phone when there is an important matter to talk about; set aside what you're doing and listen.

Have you ever had a conversation with someone who never seemed to pause, even to take a breath? I've heard many a speaker who could have been so much more effective if only he or she had learned to pause now and then for emphasis.

Have you ever listened to your pauses? Do they occur? How long are they? A one-second pause is not really a pause. It's more like taking a breath. And when you do pause, be sure you keep your eye contact. If you don't, the person may think you've stopped and jump in with what he or she wants to say. If you need to think just a bit, just hold up a finger and say, "I'm thinking for just a few seconds," and most will get the message.

If you learn to pause, your partner will see you as a person who listens. You won't feel as pressured to talk since you have more time to think of what you want to say.

Do you know when you use the pause?

After your partner has finished talking, pause to indicate that you weren't just waiting in the wings for your grand entrance onto the stage. After you've been asked a complicated or serious question, pause. This is for your benefit. You have time to think.

If you feel an argument or disagreement beginning to develop, pause and slow down. The one who slows the interchange down actually stays more in control of both the interchange as well as the outcome. You also avoid the problem of making reactionary remarks. You're less likely to be triggered by the other person's comments.[6]

Be patient, especially if your spouse is a slow or hesitant talker. You may have a tendency to jump in whenever you can find an opening, finish a statement, or hurry him along. You cannot assume that you really know what he is going to say. You can't read another's mind.

Listen to your partner with your heart and not just your head. When you listen in this way, you'll wait for your partner to share his/her thoughts and feelings, and what he or she really means.

It will do wonders for your marriage.

ENERGY BUILDERS

1. How can you listen with your eyes? Have you ever closed your eyes and listened to a person talk? Did you understand him as well as you would have if you had watched his facial features and body motion?
2. What are some of the nonverbal clues a speaker can give you? Name some ways a person can indicate that her words do not really say what she feels. How can she express boredom? Anger? Puzzlement?

7

Women Speak, Men Speak

STEP #7: BUILD A BRIDGE BETWEEN YOUR LEFT BRAIN
AND YOUR RIGHT

H*ow was your day?"*
      "Oh, it was fine. You know, typical."
"Well, what went on?"
"Nothing much. Taught the classes and graded papers."
"Oh. . . . Well, I had an interesting day. Want to hear about it?"
He looks at his watch and says, "Well. . . ."
"You know I had this appointment I've been trying to get to
for weeks and Sue was supposed to pick me up at nine o'clock and
take me there, but she didn't get here until 9:15. Never gave a reason for being late and I rushed to get ready. In fact, I couldn't find
my new taupe shoes that I wanted to wear—you don't suppose
that Tommy or the dog took them? Anyway when I got there I
ran into Rachel—haven't seen her for two years—you remember
her, I know—cute nose, but kind of shy and doesn't say much
when I'm around—anyway, she delayed me, too, and I forgot to
eat breakfast so I grabbed a donut and it was terrible. I don't
know how anyone can eat those. . . . Tony. . . . Tony! Your eyes
have that stare in them again—are you listening to me?"
Whoa—is this a typical male-female conversation or is it an

out-of-the-ordinary dialogue? Are there really "female talk" and "male talk," or is that a myth? Why are books like *Men Are from Mars and Women Are from Venus* so popular and so abundant? Because male and female talk do exist.

Women do speak a different language than men. It's not Spanish or French or Swahili. It's not Hindi or Hebrew. It's *Woman*, and it's spoken all over the planet. Men have a language of their own as well. The truth is that each speaks his or her own unique dialect. It's just another facet of learning the other's language and how to speak it.

Years ago, most of us learned to drive a car. Many, many years ago most learned on stick shifts since few cars had automatic transmissions. The gearshift was on the steering column or on the floor. It was tricky to learn to coordinate pushing the clutch as you shifted from one gear to the next. If you did it right, it went smoothly and quietly. If not, you ground the gears. You could hear as well as feel the metal clashing and grinding. And even those outside the car who heard the noise gave a knowing look. If you did this often enough, you'd grind the gears into minute pieces of metal, eventually ruining the transmission.

The same thing can happen to a man and woman as they attempt to become compatible. (Remember—no one who marries is really compatible to begin with. You grow into it.) You can end up grinding and clashing against one another. Aside from the previously discussed areas in which meshing needs to occur, another major issue comes into play when you seek to learn each other's culture—the blending of your gender and personality differences. This is a major step in learning to speak your spouse's language.

Too often we hear gender differences reduced to one factor. "It's his personality" or "She's just too right-brained" or "He's so left-brained he walks in a circle." It actually makes more sense to look at men and women as complex mixtures of differences. And let's not blame culture or upbringing.

Just as I had to learn to drive and get the gears in sync, when a man and woman are in sync, the gears don't grind as they shift in a relationship. And that's when the communication between the two comes alive.

THE DIFFERENCES ARE INNATE

To make this happen, a husband and wife need to accept the facts: men and women *are* wired differently. This is apparent in the way they talk. Neither is wired *wrong*. Women are "women" and men are "men" because the brains inside their heads are different. How are they different? We'll get to that fact later.

Several years ago, my wife and I had an experience that dramatically portrayed gender differences in both thinking and communication style. We were visiting historical Williamsburg in Virginia, a fascinating and charming setting that preserves our colonial history.

When we took the tour of the old governor's mansion, our tour guide was a male. As we entered the large entry door, he began to give a factual description of the purpose of the room as well as the way it was furnished. He described in detail the various ancient guns on the wall and pointed to the unique display of flintlock rifles arranged in a circle on the rounded ceiling. When he said there were sixty-four of them, some originals and others replicas, I immediately began counting them (which is a typical male response—we're into numbers). The guide was knowledgeable and gave an excellent detailed description as we went from room to room. He seemed to be very structured and focused.

We had to leave before the tour was completed to meet friends for lunch. Because we both enjoyed the presentation so much, we decided to return the next day and repeat the tour. But what a difference! Now our guide was a woman. We entered the same room and she said, "Now you'll notice a few guns on the wall and ceiling, but notice the covering on these chairs and the tapestry on the walls. They are. . . ." And with that she launched into a detailed description of items that had either been ignored or just given a passing mention the day before. And on it went throughout the tour.

It didn't take much to figure out what was going on. It was a classic example of gender differences. The first tour guide was speaking more to men and the second was speaking more to women. Actually, we ended up with the best tour imaginable because we heard both perspectives. What a benefit it would have been for the tourists if the guides had incorporated both of their perspectives into their presentations. Are there problems between men and women because of communication differences? Definitely.

We've asked men and women in marriage seminars all over the country to identify what frustrates them about the communication of the opposite sex. Here's a listing of some of the responses.

WHAT WOMEN SAID ABOUT MEN

• They don't share their feelings or emotions enough. It's as if they grew up emotionally handicapped.

• They seem to go into a trance when they're watching sports or when I bring up certain subjects. They're not able to handle more than one task or subject at a time.

• Men seem to think they can do things better, even when they can't. And they don't take any advice, even if it helps them.

• They don't listen well. They're always trying to fix our problems.

• Men need more intuition—get off the factual bandwagon.

• Men need to learn to enjoy shopping the way we do. They just don't know what they're missing.

• Men need more sensitivity, concern, compassion, and empathy.

• I wish men weren't so threatened by women's ideas and perspectives.

• They're so overinvolved in their work and careers. They want a family, but they don't get involved.

• Sex—that's the key word. Don't they think about anything else? They're like a microwave oven. Push the button and they're cookin'. Their "on" button is never "off."

Did you catch the different words? *Feelings, trance, listing, facts, threatened, work, sex.*

What about men? What frustrates them about women? It's generally the opposite of what women say frustrates them about men.

What Men Said about Women

• They're too emotional. They need to be more logical.

• How can they spend so much time talking? When it's said, it's said. So many of them are expanders. I wish they'd get to the bottom line quicker and at least identify the subject!

• They're too sensitive. They're always getting their feelings hurt.

• Why do they cry so easily? It doesn't make sense to me.

• I think most women are shopaholics. Their eyes glaze over when they see a shopping mall.

• They're so changeable. I wish they'd make up their minds and then keep them made up.

• Maybe they think we can read minds, but we can't. I don't think they can either.

• What's wrong with the sex drive? Sex is great.

• They think they have a gift of changing men. They ought to quit. We can't be fixed and we don't need to be!

- They're so involved with other people and their problems.
- Women are moody and negative. You can't satisfy them.
- I wish they would leave some things alone. They're always trying to fix something that isn't broken.

The words the men used? *Emotions, talking, sensitivity, shopping, changeable.*

Are these isolated comments? Not at all. I've asked this question of thousands of men and women in marriage seminars throughout the country over the past twenty-five years (that's a quarter of a century!). The responses became so predictable I could ask the question and then sit and write out what I would hear before the groups reported back with their answers.

NEITHER GENDER IS RIGHT OR WRONG

As we consider some of the unique characteristics of men and women, keep two things in mind. First, there are some generalizations that pertain to most men and women. But there will always be some exceptions. Second, the characteristics unique to men and women are not negative. It is not a fault to be either way. Certain characteristics will be more pronounced in some because of some personality types as well as upbringing. So what's the problem? It's when one feels he's always right or the way she does things is the *only* right way. There's little concern about understanding and accepting the opposite sex the way they are. The more flexibility a person develops, the more his or her marriage will benefit.[1]

It's not always easy to flex. It takes effort to learn to respond differently. But it's possible. You need to make a conscious effort to understand what's second nature for your spouse and for you.

I've talked to many men and women who say they know about the differences between the sexes, such as feeling versus fact, brain differences, energy levels, and so on. But the way they communicate leads me to ask: "If you know so much about the differences, why do you keep fighting something that's a natural and inherited difference?"

For years I've believed if couples really knew the differences between male and female styles of thinking and communicating, they'd be able to accept them and connect better. They'd honor the differences and respond appropriately and with acceptance. And it does happen. So get ready.

RIGHT BRAIN VS. LEFT BRAIN

The following may seem like a basic course in biology, physiology, and anthropology all lumped together. It really isn't. It's simply an explanation of some basic gender distinctions that continue to confuse many as well as dictate their response to their spouses.

Males are "male" and females are "female." Again, it's not just because of their physical anatomy, but because their brains are profoundly different. And yes, all men and all women *do* have brains. That's a fact, regardless of some of your experiences.

You have a left and a right hemisphere in your brain. The left controls language and reading skills. Think of it as a reporter gathering information and processing it logically in a step-by-step fashion. No editorializing. Just the facts. When do you use your left brain? When you read a book or article, play a game, sing, write, balance your checkbook, and weigh the advantages and disadvantages of buying an item on time versus paying cash.

If you're planning your day's schedule, you may decide it'd be a good idea to leave ten minutes early to drop off the DVD you rented the night before. So you plan the route that will enable you to park right in front of the store. How did you make these decisions? By using the left portion of your brain. It keeps your life sensible, organized, and on schedule. It's like a computer. Some individuals are more left-brain oriented.

And then we have the right side of your brain. That portion comes into play when you work a jigsaw puzzle, look at a road map, design a new office, plan a room arrangement, solve a geometrical problem, or listen to musical selections on the stereo. The right half of your brain doesn't process information step-by-step like the left portion. Instead, it processes patterns. It plays host to our emotions. It has been called the *intuitive side of the brain*. It links facts together and comes up with a concept. It looks at the whole situation and, as though by magic, the solution appears. It's like a kaleidoscope.

To summarize, the thinking pattern for the left side of your brain is analytical, linear, explicit, sequential, verbal, concrete, rational, and goal-oriented. Your right side is spontaneous, emotional, nonverbal, visual, artistic, holistic, and spatial. Women excel in the emotional, visual, and artistic while men excel in the spatial.

THE DOMINANT HEMISPHERE

If you're more right-side oriented and your spouse is left-side oriented, how's your communication? It's as though you speak different languages! And you do.

Ever been in a class or seminar where the presenter focused on dry, detailed facts? I mean, *really* boring. If so, you probably began to drop off. If the speaker was inflexible, he was annoyed by any interruptions. So to make matters worse and prolong the agony, after each distraction he'd return to the beginning and review. The step-by-step speech was monotonous. It was sterile. It had little emotional expression. If you've experienced this, you were listening (hopefully) to someone who was an extreme—and I mean extreme—left-brain dominant.

But if you hear a speaker or someone in a conversation who rambles from topic to topic, relies on his or her own opinion and feelings, is easily led away from the point, leaves gaps in the presentation to give the conclusion, and uses emotional language and hunches, you're in the presence of an extreme right-brain dominant. The left side says, "Come on, get to the point. What's the bottom line?" But the right side travels around the barn a few times to get there. And we've already seen that personality differences affect how a person responds.

Remember back when you were in school? You probably ran into those who excelled in math or reading but flunked playground! Why? They functioned with a highly advanced left brain but something else was less developed. What was it? Their right brain.

Meet Dave. He's a proficient chemist but also enjoys social activities twice a week. Which portion of his brain is he using for the different tasks? He uses the left side for his work. He has to be careful, accurate, and logical. But with dancing it's another story. He feels the steps by shifting to the right side of his brain. It's true he may be more comfortable using his left side, but he's able to make a switch for some right-brain activities. You and I shift back and forth between these two sides of the brain as we carry on our daily activities.

Remember, you and I will constantly reinforce our dominant side. It's easier to go that route than to break new ground by using the less-dominant side.

ALL BRAINS ARE EQUAL

Let's assume you have X-ray glasses that allow you to look into your brain and your spouse's. As you do, you may see a discrepancy. (And don't say, "I knew it. I just knew something was wrong there!")

In your brain, a bundle of nerves connects the left and right hemispheres (the technical name is *corpus caollosum*). To illustrate these differences we're going to call on Fred and Wilma, each of whom represents his or her gender. Wilma has up to 40 percent more nerves linking the two sides of her brain than Fred. (Take a look at the diagram.) This means she's able to use both sides of her brain together at one time, whereas Fred has to switch from one side of his brain to the other, depending upon what he needs. Wilma enjoys more cross-talk between both sides of her brain. And she uses all her brain at one time.

Men
Single-Minded

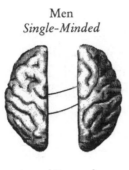

and Focused

Women
Juggler

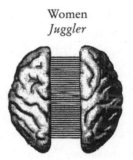

Extra connective tissue. Why they display language skills earlier. They read better—the brain that will read better is the brain that can use both sides at once.

The extra connective tissue in Wilma explains why she developed language skills earlier than Fred and will use many more words than he will. Why does Fred tend to read more poorly than Wilma? It's the brain again. *The brain that will read better is the brain that can use both sides at once.* Interestingly, it's also easier to "read" the emotions on a person's face when you use both sides of your brain simultaneously.

Wilma's brain has been developed to express and verbalize. This is why throughout adulthood she wants to "talk about it." But Fred's brain has been geared to developing his spatial skills.

That's why throughout his life he wants to "do something" about it. And that's why Wilma is usually quicker to talk about her feelings, while Fred wants to act quickly to *do* something about them.

Of course you recognize this is where conflicts arise (and probably always will). Wilma says, "Let's sit down and talk this through." Meanwhile, Fred is straining at the bit to get it fixed and get on with life. Remember: *neither response is wrong, and neither is better than the other.*

Where am I coming up with this stuff? Well, it's based on facts.

In studies at the University of Pennsylvania, brain-scan equipment has been used to generate computer photographs of brains in use. They look almost like maps. The equipment produces pictures of the brain in different colors, with each color showing a different degree of intense cortical activity.

To get this mapping, Fred and Wilma are hooked up to the equipment and they're both asked to do a spatial task: figure out how two objects fit together. If you were looking at a computer screen depicting Wilma's brain, you'd see that the color and intensity on both sides are fairly equal. But something else happens to Fred's brain. His right side lights up with various colors that reflect a *high* degree of right-brain activity and much *less* activity in the left hemisphere. But when verbal skills are tested, watch out! The difference is really apparent. Fred uses much less of his brain compared to Wilma's. Her left brain really lights up!

In a seminar, I had opportunity to see such pictures. Wilma's brain scan showed activity on both sides of the brain when she was talking. When Fred was talking, the brain scan indicated activity more on the left side.

The findings of this research indicate that a woman's brain is at work in more selections than the man's. It's as if both hemispheres are always on call, whereas in a man's brain, one hemisphere at a time is on call. A woman's brain doesn't rest the same way a man's does. Men take more mental naps than women do.

Researchers have now learned that a woman's brain has 15 percent more blood flow than a man's.[2]

Think of it like this: if there's a task to do, Fred's brain turns on. When the task is completed, his brain turns off. (I can just hear the comments about this!) But Wilma's brain is always on. It's true that parts of Fred's brain are always on, but when the two brains are compared in their downtime or inactive periods, the difference between the portion of Wilma's brain that is always on and Fred's that manifests an on/off function is quite pronounced.[3]

There are other results of the fact that women have 40 percent more, and thicker, nerve connectors between the two sides of the brain.

SPAGHETTI AND WAFFLES DO MIX!

Friends of mine have a unique way of describing these differences. They say men are like waffles and women are like spaghetti. This is what they wrote:

> Men process life in boxes. If you look down at a waffle, you see a collection of boxes separated by walls. The boxes are all separate from each other and make convenient holding places. That is typically how a man processes life. Our thinking is divided up into boxes that have room for one issue and one issue only. The first issue of life goes in the first box, the second goes in the second box, and so on. The typical man lives in one box at a time and one box only. When a man is at work, he is at work. When he is in the garage tinkering around, he is in the garage tinkering. When he is watching TV, he is simply watching TV. That is why he looks as though he is in a trance and can ignore everything else going on around him. Social scientists call this "compartmentalizing"—

that is, putting life and responsibilities into different compartments.[4]

In contrast to men's waffle-like approach, women process life more like a plate of pasta. If you look at a plate of spaghetti, you notice that there are lots of individual noodles that all touch one another. If you attempted to follow one noodle around the plate, you would intersect a lot of noodles, and you might even switch to another noodle seamlessly. That is how women face life. Every thought and issue are connected to every other thought and issue in some way. Life is much more of a process for women than it is for men.

Not all the boxes in a man's waffle brain have words. They may have thoughts and memories tucked away but they were never translated into words. Because of this, he can't communicate these experiences to others, so guess who ends up feeling left out!

There are actually some boxes that are empty. Nothing is there. And sometimes to relieve the stress in his life, he will "park" in a box to relax. There's a blank look on his face and when his wife asks, "What are you thinking?" she hears "Nothing." And it's true, though to her it's hard to believe.

And can you imagine what happens in a conversation? A husband moves from box to box and, all of a sudden, passes through a blank one. Nothing is said. He knows he should speak but there's nothing to retrieve. So, if a husband is talking, it's important for his wife to stay in the box he's opened and not all the others that are touching because he won't follow. They may be relevant to your conversation, but wait. It's just as important for a man to learn "box shifting." Just because another box is opened doesn't mean they'll all be opened—this is a fear for most men—the conversation will go on and on with no end in sight.[5]

This is why Wilma is better at multitasking than Fred is. She can tune in to everything going on around her. She may handle five hectic activities at one time while Fred is reading a magazine, oblivious to the various problems going on right under his nose. Wilma can juggle more items but can also be distracted more easily. Fred can focus on one task more effectively but lose sight of other aspects. It's like a radar lock onto a target. He has to stop one activity in order to attend to another.

MORE GENDER DIFFERENCES

Another result of this difference causes Wilma to be more perceptive than men about people. She has a greater ability to pick up feelings and sense the difference between what people say and what they mean. And Wilma's intuition has a physical basis. Her brain is like a computer that can integrate reason and intuition.

This drives some men crazy. There are numerous stories about couples who were out socially and the wife said to her husband, "I think there's a problem" or "Something is going on." Her husband responded, "How do you know? Where are the facts?" And his wife said, "I don't have any facts. I just sense it." He responds, "You don't know what you're talking about." But a week later, when he finds out she was right, he's amazed and even more puzzled.

It could be that Wilma picks up more information than Fred does since her sensitivities, such as hearing, eyesight, sense of taste, and smell, are more heightened than his. My wife, Joyce, will ask, "Don't you smell that?" and my response is, "Smell what?" She'll ask, "Doesn't this taste old to you?" and my response is "It tastes like it always has." And she'll throw it out.

The hearing difference is noted even in childhood. Fred, like most men, hears better in one ear. Wilma, like most women, hears more data and hears equally well in both ears. All the way through life, males hear less than females say. (Men are probably saying, "What?" and women, "Yes!") What does this difference do to a relationship?

It has been noted that from very early on, boys ignore voices, even parents' voices, more than girls do. Why? In some of these cases the boys are simply not hearing. They are also less proficient than girls at picking out background noises among sounds. This is one of the reasons parents, and anyone around a boy, often say they have to speak louder to the boy than to a girl.[6]

What does this difference mean? It's the main reason Fred is a fixer, task-oriented, and not as able to do several things at once. He's got to focus on one thing at a time. When Fred takes on a task at home, such as cleaning the garage or working in the yard, to him it's a single-focus task, *not a conversation time*. If Wilma wants to work with him, she usually wants to carry on a conversation simultaneously. To him this may seem an interruption, an invasion of his space, a distraction, and he reacts strongly to it. Millions and perhaps billions of conflicts over the years could have been avoided if men and women had not only understood this but honored the difference.

When there's an overload of words, a man presses the mute button. Talking may continue, but it isn't heard.

WHEN DIFFERENCES COLLIDE

Generally speaking, when it comes to approaching and solving problems, Wilma uses both sides of her brain and is able to create an overview. But Fred tends to break the problem down into pieces in order to come up with a solution. He goes through steps 1, 2, 3, and 4 and has a solution. It's a linear approach. Wilma tends to go through steps 1, 3, 2, 5, and 4 and reaches the same conclusion. If she arrives there before he does, Fred probably won't accept her correct answer because he hasn't completed Steps 1, 2, 3, and 4 yet. Why? He's not ready for her answer.

Wilma tends to feel that Fred isn't listening. He is, but he's not ready. So she complains, "It's obvious! Why can't you see it?" He can't see it because that's *not* the way he thinks.

Fred says, "Just take it one step at a time—you can't approach it that way." But Wilma can. Neither is wrong, they're just different. Can you imagine what they (and all couples) could accomplish if they learned to use each other's creativity and strength?[7]

Fred likes structure. He and other men like to put things in order. They like to regulate, organize, enumerate (men love to talk about numbers and statistics), and fit things into rules and patterns. It's not unusual for them to take the time to put their CDs and videos in alphabetical order or to figure out how long it takes to walk two miles or drive eighty-five miles to their favorite fishing hole.

Ever wonder why some men like Fred have a set routine on Saturday? Maybe the order is wash the car, mow the lawn, trim the roses, and take a nap. And he always does it at the same time in the same order.[8] Order provides structure and conserves energy. Keep the word *energy* in mind, for it's the source of contention between men and women.

The way in which Fred uses his brain is an exclusive mode. (Wilma often refers to it as "tunnel vision"!) It can exclude everything except what he is focusing on. It shuts out other possibilities. Remember—it's a radar lock. And Fred exerts an abundance of energy to stay in this position. Fred and most men like to know exactly where they are and what they are doing at a given point in time. It's a way to stay in control.

So, when Fred is at home and his attention is locked onto the TV, the newspaper, or fixing the car, he's in his exclusive mind-set. The radar lock is on! If Wilma talks to him, he feels an interference or intrusion. *And for him it's an energy leak.* He hopes it will leave. When he does exert energy to shift from whatever he was doing to concentrate on his wife, he's upset because of the energy expenditure. He has to change his focus and shift it elsewhere because he can't handle both at once.

What does she feel? *He's inconsiderate for not listening.* What about him? Fred feels she's inconsiderate because of the intrusion. Actually, neither is. They just don't understand the gender difference. If they did, they could each learn to respond differently.

Wilma is inclusive and can jump in and out of different topics. There's no energy drain for her. She actually picks up energy by entering into new experiences and changes. She is able to see the situation and beyond. Wilma sees and responds to life like a camera with a wide-angle lens, whereas Fred's camera has a highly focused microscope lens. He sees the tree in great detail; she senses the tree, but she also sees the grove and its potential. Woman's expectation of a man's perceptual ability should be tempered with this knowledge.[9]

Remember, there will be exceptions to what I'm saying here. Some men and women will be just the opposite. My wife and I are exceptions. I tend to be the juggler and she is more single-minded, and it appears that personality preference (which I discuss in other chapters) has a modifying effect on some of these characteristics.

Here's another issue: since Fred focuses on one thing at a time and Wilma can handle several things, if she's doing two or three things while talking to him, he feels she's not paying attention to him. In his mind he thinks, *If she were interested, she'd look at me with 100 percent attention.* Here's another example that's been expressed many times:

Men also can't understand how women can leave the theater or the living room during the most important part of a movie to go to the bathroom. A man will hold it! He has his priorities. He also has a larger bladder! On the other hand, the woman's "inclusive" mode gives her a sense of what's going on in the film, and she can still "watch" the film while she's in the bathroom. If the man is not physically watching the movie, he misses out. Even though she may not have caught all the details, she doesn't have a sense of missing anything.[10]

Sound familiar?

WHY MEN SEEM SO UNEMOTIONAL

This brings us to a question that you've probably heard again and again over the years: *why can't men get into feelings like a woman does*? The answer is that men have three strikes against them when it comes to feelings.

One, they're wired differently.

Two, they're raised to be emotionally handicapped. They're given neither the encouragement nor the training to learn to understand a wide range of feelings, nor to develop a vocabulary to express them. By the way, men and women do not have different emotions. The way men and women deal with and express emotions may be different.

Three, the way women respond to men to get to their feelings often becomes counterproductive. Pressuring or even asking a man "How do you feel?" usually doesn't work.

Remember Fred and Wilma and the discussion about their brain differences? Wilma has an immense number of neuroconnectors between her feelings and the "broadcasting studio" in her brain. She has an expressway that runs between her feelings and her speech. And remember, since her brain is on all the time, it's easy for her to share these feelings.

On the other hand, remember that Fred's brain has fewer nerve connectors between its right and left sides. No wonder, then, that he often has more of a struggle than Wilma in expressing feelings. He doesn't have an expressway between feelings and the broadcasting area of the brain. It's more of a one-way road and narrow at that.[11]

This is why it isn't easy for Fred to share. If he attempts to put his feelings into words, he has to take a preliminary step called *thought*. He has to say, *Now I'm feeling something. What is it? All right, that's what it is*. Once he discovers the feelings, he's got to analyze them and decide what he can do about them.

GENDERLECTS AND GENDERFLEX

To what extent does the previous description fit your spouse?

How will what you just read help you in responding to your spouse?

This whole business of relationships is about left-brained men and right-brained women being attracted to each other. If they're ever going to communicate across their natural gender gap, if they are to develop into a functional couple, they need to learn to understand and use the other's language style to some extent. They must become "bilingual." Can you make this switch? Can your spouse?

The differences we have outlined between the brains of men and women mean that when they communicate (or attempt to) they have different purposes in mind. Women speak and hear a language of connection and intimacy, whereas a man tends to speak and hear a language of status and independence. Do *you* hear this in the words and phrases you use?

The way men speak is *report talk*. They like to express knowledge and skills. They use talking as a way to get and keep attention.

Women's speech is *rapport talk*. It's their way of establishing connections and negotiating relationships. Solutions are secondary and connections are first.

So what you have is not really a difference of dialects within the same language, but cross-cultural communication. It's been said that men and women speak different *genderlects*.[12]

This area of difference is not just a concern in marriage but in the workplace as well: "The male-female difference represents the biggest culture gap that exists. If you can learn the skills and attitudes to bridge the gender differences in communication, you will have mastered what it takes to communicate and negotiate *with* almost anyone *about* almost anything."[13]

There's a new word floating around. It's *genderflex*, and it's been coined for this situation. It's not in the dictionary yet, but it will be. The word means to temporarily use communication patterns typical of the other gender in order to connect with them and increase the potential for influence.[14]

This is just a simple approach to communication designed to improve relationships and performance. *It isn't a change in personality, lifestyle, or values*. It's learning to speak another language, and it's so simple! It's learning to adapt in a way that will actually create greater flexibility and growth between those practicing it. You choose to communicate in the patterns of the other gender to accomplish a goal. You simply adopt the communication characteristics of the other's gender that are related to style, content, and structure of communication. You're not becoming like the other gender but showing that you understand how that gender communicates.

Those who use genderflex talk will remember that women tend to speak the language of *expressers* and men the language of *resolvers*. A simple example of this is that typically most women are *expanders* and most men are *condensers* of the content they share. We've discussed this elsewhere. Women tend to give much more detail and include feelings in what they share, whereas men tend to give bottom-line, factual information.

So, to speak your spouse's language, even if you (if you're a woman) were talking about interpersonal situations, use more factual descriptions that focus on identifying a problem or a solution rather than an abundance of details or feelings. And if you're a man, don't give just the bottom-line facts but descriptive details with an emphasis on the interpersonal.[15] We men tend to edit in our minds. We think, *Nah, that detail is not important*. But every time we think that, it means it probably *is* important to a woman and we need to say it.

Keep in mind that you will find exceptions to these male-female styles. Some men and women will express themselves just the opposite from the ways I've described. This is probably due to the influence of personality variation.

WOMENSPEAK AND MENSPEAK

Many men will say they prefer talking to women because women are better at conversation. What women are actually better at are listening and the art of supporting the other person's conversational efforts, encouraging him to go on, enabling him to explain fully, and reinforcing his conversational efforts with smiles, head nods, good eye contact, and other indications of attentiveness.

Certain words and categories of words appear much more frequently in women's speech than in men's. Adverbs of intensity (such as *awfully, terribly, pretty, quite, so,* and the adjectives *charming, lovely, adorable, divine, cute,* and *sweet*) are more common in women's usage.

Women also have a much more extensive vocabulary for colors than men. Words for colors like *taupe, beige, mauve, lavender,* and *violet* are not common in men's speech. Males are not expected to discuss the "lovely mauve drapes" in the conference room, or the "streaks of lavender" in the sunset.

Recently I was looking at the book entitled *Genderflex*. Even in this book written about male-female communication, the wording of the titles for each gender was significantly different. A title for one chapter was: "Women's Communication—What to Enhance, Improve, Delete," which contained guidelines for communicating with men. Another chapter contained guidelines for men to connect with women and was entitled, "Men's Communication—What to Keep, Add, Delete." Notice the differences?

It's significant since the wording reflects words that either gender would tend to use. Listen to the wording of your spouse. See his or her words as windows of opportunity to expand your vocabulary and enter your spouse's world.

Men and women have been taught to use language differently. For women, speech communication is basically for social relationships. Women have been raised to use communication as a mechanism for creating bonds. Men have been encouraged to communicate primarily to exchange information.

Men tend to feel more comfortable speaking in public than in private, intimate conversations. With most women it's just the opposite. Women enjoy private, one-on-one conversations because they are more personal, intimate, and they build relationships. Most men use conversation to gain status, to negotiate and to solve problems, to get attention, and even to keep their independence.[16]

I've heard both men and women say, "Why should I go to all this work of adapting and changing? If my partner would talk less [or talk more] and listen, everything would be all right." There's a better question to ask: "Is what you are doing to communicate working?" If not, then why keep doing it? There's a better way.[17]

ENERGY BUILDERS

1. Describe how you and your spouse differ in your communication style.

2. What frustrates you or concerns you about your spouse's communication style?

3. How do you wish your spouse would communicate differently?

4. What will *you* do to help the process?

5. In light of this information, how will you respond differently to your spouse?

6. In light of this information, how would you like your spouse to respond to you?

8

Translate and You'll Connect
STEP #8: CHANGE YOUR WORDS TO WHAT
WORKS FOR YOUR SPOUSE

Nathan: I just don't see why we have to go to that meeting.

Amy: I've told you several times. How many more times do I need to tell you?

Nathan: I just can't picture why it's so vital that I go.

Amy: But I've told you again and again. Don't you listen to me?

Nathan: I just think it's kind of shortsighted of you to give me two days' notice. I was looking forward to doing something else that day.

Amy: What are you saying, Nathan?

Nathan: Don't you understand? Can't you see that I'm already tied up?

Miscommunication? Perhaps. Not listening? Possibly. Defensiveness? Well ... what about all of the above? It could be, but even more than all of these issues, what about speaking two different languages?

Let's consider this same situation from a different direction.

Three women were talking. One said to the others, "Anyone knows that seeing is believing."

The woman next to her turned and said, "Oh, no, hearing is believing."

"I hate to inform you," the third one countered, "but you're both wrong. Feeling is believing."

Who's right? Who's wrong in this discussion? They *all* are. For some seeing is believing, for others hearing is, and for a third group, feeling or sensing is believing.

How do you respond, and how does your spouse respond, to life? Do you *see* things more? Do you *hear* things more? Do you *sense* or *feel* things more? Our perception of the world around us is created through our visual, auditory, kinesthetic (or feeling), and our olfactory/gustatory (smell and taste) senses. Because of the influences upon us and our experiences with our environment, we tend to develop or lean upon one of these senses or intake systems more than the others. We use them all, but we rely more heavily upon one of them. And this affects the way we talk and listen.

THREE TYPES OF LEARNING STYLES

You may be an auditorally oriented husband or wife. You tend to depend upon spoken words for your information. If you're visually oriented, you use your eyes to perceive your world, and you use visual images in remembering and thinking. If you're a kinesthetically oriented individual, you tend to feel your way through your experiences. Your feelings sort both what you experience inside as well as what comes at you from the outside, and these feelings determine your decisions. In our culture, very few people rely just upon smell and taste.

Auditory

An auditory man or woman wants to hear about life. This is how he or she learns best, and it's been suggested that 20 percent of our population falls into this learning style.

When I was in junior high school, I remember the band and orchestra members took auditory tests each year. We listened to various tones and pitches to determine our ability. Some students made some very fine auditory distinctions; these individuals had an auditory bent or inclination. We were allowed to sing in the class choir. The others were taught to lip-sync the words. The intake system we use affects the way we respond to and cope with life.

Is this anyone you know?

Visual

A visual man (or woman) relates to the world around him in terms of how things look. This is how he learns best, and it's been suggested that 60 to 70 percent of people are visual. When he imagines he visualizes, and when he remembers, he recalls a picture. He experiences life through his eyes. He's primarily a watcher: movies, TV, sporting events, people, art exhibits or museums, scenery. He probably prefers reading, collecting items to look at, taking pictures, and looking at you. He's often concerned with how he looks to others. A visual person talks about how things look rather than how he feels. Often he tends to withdraw and brood when upset rather than talking through the problem. Is this anyone you know?

My visual side frequently comes to the forefront. If one of my coworkers comes into my office and says, "Norm, here's an interesting letter. Let me read it to you." Without thinking I'll respond, "Oh, let me see it." I like to read things because I process them faster that way. Invariably I ask people to "send it to me in writing," or "Put your suggestions down in writing and turn them in so I can see them."

Recently I heard the story of several office employees who felt frustrated about getting their requests and ideas across to the vice president. They approached the man and talked with him, and at times he appeared interested, but nothing ever came of their meetings with him. When three of these employees discussed the problem with their office manager, he made a simple suggestion: "It isn't as though your ideas don't have merit. They're just not registering with him. I think he's a person who, like it or not, needs everything to come to his attention in writing. I know this means a little extra work for you, but let's try presenting everything in a written format. This doesn't mean that you can't share your ideas in person, but at the same time have it typed out in detail, and let's see what happens."

They grumbled a bit but followed the suggestion. Were they surprised when their ideas, which their boss had apparently discarded before, were accepted! Why? Because the vice president is visual and likes to have his information in writing. When his employees began to talk his language, he began to listen.

When I, a visual, hear new ideas or concepts, whether they are simple or complex, I begin to think, *How can I diagram these concepts and put them on PowerPoint so I can convey them better to those I teach?*

Kinesthetic (Feelings)

Some tend to be very feeling-oriented, although it's often more true of women than men. (When it comes to learning, only about 10 percent fall into this learning style even though many more are very feeling-oriented. Thus a visual person can still be very feeling.) Feeling-oriented people tend to touch. Often they desire to develop deep relationships. They crave closeness, love, and affection. They're generally right-brain people, operating more intensely than logically or analytically. Physical comfort and bodily sensations are important parts of their language style.

Feeling-oriented people often show their feelings even though many don't verbalize them well. You can usually read happiness, sadness, anger, love, or delight on their faces. And they're concerned about how others feel toward them. A feeling-oriented man who can effectively verbalize his emotions can be one of the easiest husbands to live with.

Feeling-oriented individuals are more spontaneous than auditory or visual people. This trait can be both positive and negative. On one hand, they're free to create spur-of-the-moment fun activities. On the other hand, they may, for no apparent logical reason, change their minds and upset the schedule of a plan-in-advance spouse. Anyone you know?

WORD CHOICES REVEAL YOUR LEARNING STYLE

Let's summarize what I have been *saying* to *see* if you're in *touch* with it yet. (Notice I used words for all three senses.) We have three main senses—hearing, seeing, and feeling. We prefer one over the other two for perceiving life, storing our experiences, and making decisions. How do we discover which sense we prefer? Our *language* gives it away.

A Visual's Choice of Words
A visual spouse uses terms like:

> I *see* what you're saying.
> That *looks* good to me.
> I'm not too *clear* on this right now.
> This is still a bit *hazy* to me.
> When they asked that question, I just went *blank*.
> That sheds a new *light* on the problem.
> Do you pick up my *perspective*?

Here are some of the most typical words you'll hear from a visual spouse:

focus	colorful	see	pretty
clear	peek	bright	glimpse
picture	imagine	perspective	notice
show	color	hazy	

If you've identified your spouse as a visual, practice using visually oriented words, especially if they're new to you. Write down a list of these words—as many as possible—and look for ways to use them in conversation with your visually oriented partner. If you usually say, "That feels good to me," change to "That looks good to me" when you are talking. At first you'll feel awkward as you try out a new vocabulary. Continue to practice and you'll soon feel at ease. This is the first step in connecting with your spouse's language style.

But don't expect your spouse to notice your change in vocabulary. He or she probably won't be aware of a language switch. But what's amazing is that your spouse will feel more comfortable relating to you, perhaps without even knowing why.

Men tend to be more visual than women; in fact, most men are visual. In our society, women tend to lean toward feelings. But both can learn to strengthen the two senses that are subordinate to the dominant language.

Even though we have a dominant sense, we may increase our use of the others. For a number of reasons I've learned to do this over the years. My primary sensing apparatus has been visual. That's my bent. It was emphasized and reinforced when I was a child. I read extensively, and perhaps that helped create the imaginative pictures in my mind. I also learned to sight-read music quite well between the ages of six and twelve. At times I'm still frustrated by those who can't read a note of music, but if you hum a tune for them, they can play fifteen variations of that theme! My orientation is visual. Theirs is auditory. Even though the visual trait has been and still is my strong suit, I've worked on the other two and now enjoy a greater balance.

If you live with a visual, you need to adjust to his dominant style of perception. For example, if you're planning to buy new chairs for the family room, you'll want to discuss how the room's appearance will improve *in addition* to how comfortable the chairs will be. If you want to escape to a quiet retreat with no phones and few people, emphasize the scenic aspects of the location. A visual person is more responsive to certain aspects of lovemaking. Romantic décor, leaving the lights on, or making sure you wear certain apparel may be more important.

An Auditory's Choice of Words

These people relate more to sounds than sights. Reading a book, the auditory person hears words silently rather than seeing pictures. If your partner is auditory, don't expect him or her to notice a new article of clothing, hairdo, room arrangement, or plant in the yard. You need to *tell* your partner more than *show*. This spouse prefers talking about something to looking at it. Long conversations are important, and the auditory tend to remember what they hear better than others.

If you want to share feelings, the auditory spouse will best understand if you verbalize how you feel. Auditory people hear equally what is said and not said, and they're astute at picking up tonal changes and voice inflections. Harsh responses may be upsetting to them. And the telephone is an important part of their lives.

Auditory folks fall into two different categories. Some feel compelled to fill the silent moments of life with sound: talking, playing the stereo, humming. But others prefer quiet. Why would an auditory person opt for silence? Because many are carrying on internal conversations and external sounds are an interruption. Sometimes a silent auditory spouse's intermittent verbal responses may not make sense to you because he fails to relate the ongoing conversation in his head. This is especially true if he is an introvert.

Romancing an auditory person has to include saying "I love you" again and again. But how you say it is as important as how often you say it. Discover the words, phrases, and tones that best convey your spoken love and use them often.

Here are some of the words and phrases an auditory person uses:

That *sounds* good to me.
Let's *talk* about this again.
That's *music* to my ears!
People seem to *tune* him in when he's talking.
Harmony's important to me.
I *hear* you clear as a bell.
Tell me a little more about it.
Give me a *call* so we can discuss the proposal.
Your *tone* of voice is coming through loud and clear.

Here are some of the typical words you'll hear from an auditory spouse:

listen	loud	yell	shout
talk	told	hear	tone
harmony	sounds	noisy	say
discuss	amplify	call	

What kind of responses should you use with auditory people? The same type of words and phrases they use. Identify them, write them out, and practice them. A simple change from "Doesn't that look good to you?" to "Doesn't that sound good to you?" will make a difference. Instead of asking, "Would you like to go see that new movie with me?" ask "How does attending that new movie sound to you?" Asking auditory people to share their feelings may not provoke a response. But asking them to say what comes to mind when they hear the word *love, romance,* or *sexy* will tap into their auditory style. Now you're speaking their language!

After learning about these differences, a woman told me she

understood her husband better. She said, "I used to ask Grant if he couldn't see that I had too much work to do and needed his help. But it was as though that didn't register with him. All he was concerned about was the noise level around the house. He wanted the kids to quiet down and the stereo softer. After I discovered he was auditory, I realized that loud sounds bothered him more than the clutter I needed help with. I used to think he was just picky when a faucet or freeway noise bothered him at night."

Remember Nathan and Amy? Go back and reread their brief dialogue at the beginning of the chapter, and the problem may be a bit more obvious. But there's also a third group of people.

A Kinesthetic's Choice of Words
While a visual says, "It looks good to me," and the auditory says, "It sounds good to me," a feelings person will say, "It feels good to me," or "I'm comfortable with that," or "I understand how you feel."

A kinesthetic spouse uses phrases such as these:

I can't get a *handle* on this.
I've got a good *feeling* about this project.
Can you get in *touch* with what I'm saying?
It's easy to *flow* with what they're saying.
I don't *grasp* what you're trying to do.
This is a *heavy* situation.

Some of their typical words are:

feel	irritated	firm	clumsy
touch	pushy	pressure	relaxed
tense	grab	concrete	soft
hurt	handle	touchy	smooth
relaxed			

You may think, *Changing the way we talk to one another sounds like a pointless game that requires a lot of work.* Work, yes; game, no. Effective communication requires being sensitive to and accommodating the uniqueness of your partner. By learning new ways to talk, we climb out of our communication ruts and become more flexible. Changing your style of communication can make the difference between holding your spouse's attention and being ignored. Isn't that reason enough?

LEARNING TO IDENTIFY STYLES

What's your strongest sense? What is your spouse's? Had you considered this idea before? I find it easy to close my eyes and picture in my mind an experience from the past or even an anticipated experience. When I read a novel, I see the action in my mind in vivid color and can describe all the details. But this would be difficult for others. I might find it hard to experience the smell of a flower in my mind. I could work at it, but for others it would be easier. Some can hear the sounds of life all around them just by thinking. Some individuals have vivid mental images, where others have faded images and some none at all. Some of us see sentences in our minds.

As you talk with your spouse, you may even wonder which is his or her dominant sense, especially if you've never thought about this before.

How can you discover your partner's style? There are times when it really isn't apparent, and you won't know instantly which response will work best. So experiment. And the first step is to *listen*. If you're not sure which sensing mode is dominant, vary your questions. Ask, "Does this idea *look* all right to you?" "How do you *feel* about investing in this new program?" If one approach doesn't seem to work switch to the other, and if that doesn't work, try the third. Talk about it together.

Let's look at some conversations and see how the participants indicate they are *visual, kinesthetic,* or *auditory.*

Visual: Honey, if you would look over that new room arrangement again, you'll see that I've taken your needs into consideration. I've focused on the important places in the room. It looks good to me. I don't see what you're so bothered about.

Kinesthetic: I don't know. . . . I just keep getting the feeling that something about it is wrong. I've just got this sense about it. You know, I can't put my finger on it. . . . It's just a bit uncomfortable.

Visual: Oh, come on. You're just stuck in your own point of view about this. Look at it from my perspective. The room is brighter this way, and we have more walking space. Stand over here and look around the room.

Kinesthetic: I don't know. I don't think you're in touch with how I feel about this room. I just can't get a handle on it, but if we leave it this way, it just isn't going to work.

What's happening in this conversation? Well, we do have two points of view (there's my visual coming out again!). But the main problem is that they're talking right past each other. They are not connecting. One uses words referring to how he *sees* things, and the other's words reflect how she *feels.* Let's listen in on another discussion between a *visual* and an *auditory.*

Auditory: John, I want to talk with you about something that we've spoken about before. I know we're ready to move on the room addition, but I've still got some ideas, and I want to know how these sound to you. Now please hear me out, because they are a bit involved.

Visual: Well, do you have them outlined for me? Let me see them first, and then we can act on them. That will save a lot of time as well, since I've got a lot going on right now.

Auditory: Well, they're not that finalized yet. I've just started to tune into them, and I thought we could discuss them. You know, I do want to have some say in the final outcome.

Visual: Oh, I agree. You need to have your views reflected in this new addition. But for me to focus in on what you're trying to present, I would like you to have something definite to show me. Why don't you formulate it clearly, and then let's talk?

Again, miscommunication. They're talking two different languages, but if one or both could change, they would connect. It's just a matter of translating your language to the other.

Here is an example of translating with all three approaches. It can be done!

Visual: As I look over these plans for the new room arrangement you showed me, I have some questions about it. I'm just not clear where we are going to put all the old and new furniture.

Translator: Well, I think I can see where your concern is coming from. Maybe it's not all that clear to me either, but let me try to paint a picture of what's inside my head. I guess I need to illustrate this for both of us so we can discover the solution.

Auditory: John, let's talk some more about the new addition. I listened to your thoughts last night, and since I've had some time to consider them, I wonder if we're really on the same wavelength. Now, here's what I want to say.

Translator: All right, I hear you. I'll try to tune into your thoughts on this room. I want it to be comfortable for both of us. I sure want us to be in harmony over this room, since we have to live with it for the next few years.

Kinesthetic: I'm sorry, but I just can't seem to get in touch with what you're saying. It just isn't concrete enough for me to grab on to it. I want this room to feel comfortable to me and everyone else. So far what you've been describing to me just doesn't seem to fit.

Translator: Well, I understand what you're feeling. We are connecting on this, even though it doesn't feel that way for you.

This translator was able to fit his or her vocabulary to his partner's. This is a classic example of speaking the other person's language. You can act as a translator when you talk with others.

TRANSLATING OUTSIDE YOUR MARRIAGE

You can also act as a translator for two people who tend to speak different languages. Let's go back to Jan and Bill again from chapter 3. Bill said, "She keeps showing me her ideas for the wedding dinner, but they don't make sense to me. She wants it to look right, but the way it's set up now it appears to be disorganized, and there's not enough time allotted between the different events. But she can't seem to see this."

Jan chimed in at this point and said, "Bill, you're just insensitive to what's important to my family. Mom and Dad and I talked, and we feel this is the best way to have the dinner. You just can't get in touch with the fact that others do things differently, and it can work. After all, Dad is footing the bill for this part of it, too, so they have a right to be involved."

I jumped in at this point since they weren't hearing each other. "Bill, I think Jan is just trying to show you that even though you have a different perspective, it will work out. She'd like you to see it from her family's point of view. Jan, perhaps you could try to sense where Bill is coming from. Perhaps he feels a bit overwhelmed because your family is pulling together. Why not clear it up for him—then you'd end up feeling more comfortable about it?" They both seemed to hear me when I presented the solution in that manner. Their language and thinking are different. The language of feelings is different from the language of sight, and the language of sound is different from the other two.

As you listen to movies, television, teachers, or ministers, notice (there's a visual word again!) how the information is being presented to you. Some ads, lectures, sermons, or illustrations that don't appeal to you would if the person giving the presentation put it into your language. If others aren't responding to us, perhaps it's because we are not putting our responses into *their* language!

WHEN STYLES CLASH

If a visual woman marries an auditory man, the husband may not meet his wife's standards for dressing since he's less concerned with fashion. And his wife may tend more toward neatness and orderliness in the household because of its visual attractiveness. An auditory husband may forget the visible shopping list his wife gives him but will have better success remembering verbal lists and instructions.

What if the husband is visual and the wife is auditory? He attempts to show his love by buying her flowers and gifts and taking her places. Then one day she says, "You don't love me," and he's floored. He points to all the things he has given her, but she simply says, "You never tell me you love me." To the auditory wife, words are more important than gifts.

The auditory wife may also err by limiting the expression of her love to her visually oriented husband to mere words. He may appreciate his wife telling him of her love, but he will really get the message when his brain receives certain visual stimuli. Her attention to grooming, dress, neatness in the home, and pleasant sights rather than sounds will visually present her love.

Sometimes people come into my work area and rearrange my personal items. These people may think I won't notice, but I do. I've also made some people uncomfortable when, in a home or a doctor's office, I'll take it upon myself to straighten a crooked picture on the wall. What does this say about me? Yes, I am more visually oriented.

Again, a feelings-oriented person needs to respond to the visual spouse by talking about how he "sees" things. The visual partner, in turn, should learn to develop a "feel" for those things that are important to his spouse.[1]

When we understand differences, we will then understand our partners' reactions, misunderstandings, annoying habits, and personality peculiarities. If our spouses' styles are different from ours, then we approach them in the appropriate language style first and *then* lead them to understand what we are saying.

For example, if your wife is visual, don't demand that she open up and respond on a feeling level. First, she has to connect with you on a visual level to feel comfortable. If your feelings are shared gradually, in a visual style, your partner will begin to relate to you. It's not always the easiest for a visual person to express his or her feelings in words.

Explain to your spouse that you can see her feelings even if she is not expressing them. Ask how things look to her first rather than how she feels. In time you can ask, "How would you express that if you were to use my feelings word?" and she just may be able to do it.

If your husband is auditory, don't expect him to notice your new outfit or that you've washed the car or cleaned the garage. He needs to hear about it first. If you want your spouse to share his feelings, remember they're triggered by what he hears. He's more tuned into words than feelings and usually carries on inner conversations with himself.

ADAPTING YOUR PRESENTATION

Does your spouse respond to your requests, or do you frequently experience frustration because nothing gets done? Are you sometimes confused as to why a "perfectly logical" request on your part meets with resistance? If so, perhaps you presented it in such a way that it doesn't make sense to your spouse. It may be it doesn't capture his or her attention because you haven't used his or her language.

Perhaps you've heard it happen in something as simple as making a suggestion about what you'd like to do for a vacation. If you don't present it according to what your spouse would enjoy doing, you could get turned down.

John had a great idea for a vacation (or so it seemed to him), but when he presented it to his wife, Joan, she appeared uninterested and negative. As he told me in a counseling session, "I can't understand her. You've suggested that we take some time together and rebuild our relationship, but when I sprang this great idea on her for a trip to Mexico, she threw cold water on it."

I replied, "John, you said you 'sprang this idea on her.' Tell me exactly how you approached her."

"Well," he said, "when I got home, I just came in the front door and yelled to her, 'Honey, I've got this great plan for a ten-day vacation for us, and we can go next month. Where are you? I want to show this to you.' And then I found her in the kitchen, getting dinner ready, and I said, 'Look at this: a ten-day vacation in Mexico at a price we can afford. Take a look at this brochure. I've checked my schedule at the office, and in five weeks I'm clear, and we can leave. Look at these pictures of the sandy beach, and the fishing there is great! They take you out in these little boats, so you don't have to fight the crowds and you're away from the busy cities. Just think: ten days to bum around the beach, barefoot, cooking fresh fish over the coals. Isn't that great?' But she didn't seem interested."

"Does Jean enjoy having you spring a surprise on her, or does she enjoy being a part of the process of selecting something?" I asked.

John thought a minute. "Hmmm . . . no, I guess she likes to be involved in looking things over and giving her input."

"All right. Can she handle a lot of information all at one time, or does she prefer to have it presented a piece at a time so she can consider it, ask questions, and think about it?"

John sat silently for a minute, then said, "Yeah, you're right. I guess I came on like a steamroller. She likes to think about things and take them a step at a time."

I continued, "You seemed to emphasize the things *you* enjoy doing. Are fishing, walking on a sandy beach, and cooking fresh fish her favorite activities on a vacation?"

John slumped in his chair, shook his head, and smiled. "Oh, my. I can see what I did. You've been telling me to approach her in a way that makes her feel comfortable, and I did the wrong thing again. Of course fishing isn't her favorite activity on a vacation. She likes to fish a couple of hours a day for two or three days, but she enjoys sightseeing and exploring new areas and shopping in new stores and visiting art galleries. Man, if I had it to do all over again, I think I'd have approached her with a few questions, to get her attention."

"John, what would some of those have been?"

He thought a moment and told me, "All right, if I were to do it over again, I would have gone home, and after we had talked about the day, I would have asked, 'Have you ever dreamed of sleeping in in the morning and then lounging under the palm trees while you ate breakfast?' If she asked why, I could have said, 'Oh, no real reason. I just thought I'd ask.' Later I'd say, 'Have you ever thought of exploring Mayan ruins with your camera to see what you could discover? How would that feel to you?' If I did that, after a while, she'd stop everything and say, 'All right, something is up. You're not just asking questions to be asking. There's a reason, and I'm curious. What are you getting at?' Then she would *want* to know. You're right. We *are* different. I approached her the way *I* would want to be approached. But I ran over her. I think I can save the day, though. I'm going to develop a new plan, and I think she'll hear me this time." His wife did hear him because of a different presentation.

How do you express your ideas to your spouse—in your language or your spouse's? Even varying the kinds of questions we use helps the other realize that we can relate to his or her world and way of responding to life.

Yes, it's true. You probably married a foreigner when it comes to communication. But any and all of us can learn to adapt and expand our ability to connect with our spouses. And you know what? It's worth the effort. And when you put your request for change into a presentation that matches the other person's uniqueness of gender, personality, communication style, and perceptual style, not only do you show respect for your spouse, but he or she will hear you.

ENERGY BUILDERS

1. What are the three forms of perception that are most common in our society? How can you tell which is the most important one in a person's life?

2. Which method of perception is your dominant one? How can you tell? Which is your spouse's?

3. How can you use pacing and perception to better your communication? How can you act as translator for two people with different methods of perception?

4. How do people use sense appeal on a daily basis? How can you use your awareness of it to present your ideas effectively to others?

9

Feelings: Where Do They Fit In?
Step #9: Develop a "Feelings" Vocabulary

They first noticed each other in a college class where they struck up a conversation. Soon they were sitting next to each other; then one day they went out to dinner. The dating process continued after graduation. They talked about everything, or so it seemed. That was ten years ago. Today, after eight years of marriage and two children, they seldom talk. Hear their story.

"When James and I were dating, we got along so well," Sheila said. "I mean, we could talk. There didn't seem to be any restrictions. My questions were always answered and Jim appeared to be interested in everything. Sure, we both knew I tended to talk more than he did, but that didn't seem to be a problem. I didn't have to push him to talk.

"A month after we married, however, our communication changed. I didn't change—he did. He began to respond with about a tenth of his previous openness, and it continues. He's become so private. I know I've made mistakes. I've pressured him and talked more. I've tried to figure him out but it hasn't worked. Did I do something wrong to turn him off? How could a man communicate so well during courtship and then pull the plug after we married? Was it a ploy to win me? I feel deceived, disappointed, and set up."

James sat in my office, looking a bit dismayed and sounding even more so as he slumped in the wingback chair. He looked up at me and, with hands open in a frustrated gesture, said, "I just don't know what to say. I realize that I'm not great at communication, but this bit about sharing my feelings puzzles me. Half the time I don't even know what I'm feeling, let alone know how to describe it. What am I? Some kind of freak?"

"You sound frustrated and confused," I responded. "But let me assure you, you're not alone in your predicament. Many, many men today are in your position. We've been told we need to share our feelings, and it would be healthier for us to do so, but it's like telling a crippled person to stand up and walk. How can we be expressive when it's something we've never been taught? Who's going to help us?"

"That's it," James said. "I feel emotionally crippled. My father never shared his emotions or feelings much, so early in life I guess I got the message that for a man to have feelings or emotions meant he was weak. So those I did experience I just stuffed, hoping they'd disappear. But others around me aren't letting me get away with that anymore. What can I do now?"

James had just asked an important question that I hear often in my practice.

Brain Differences

Remember that earlier in this book, we learned that Fred's brain is a problem-solving brain. He's wired to have delayed reactions. When an emotional event occurs, is Fred ready to express his feelings? No. He needs a brain shift. He needs to move over to the left side of his brain and collect the words he knows express his feelings. That's what stops Fred and most men from expressing emotions. They're vocabulary-deficient. I know I was through my early adult life.

And it's not all Fred's fault either. Parents, teachers, and society as a whole failed to provide much help in teaching him the vocabulary of feelings or the ability to paint word pictures to describe them. He shares what he's able to share, and when new feelings arise, it's back to the drawing board to start the process all over again.

So remember this difference: *A man has to think about his feelings before he can share them. A woman can feel, talk, and think at the same time.*[1]

The sequence Fred's wife, Wilma, goes through is quite different. When she's upset, what does she do first? She talks about it. And as she talks she is able to think about what she is saying and feeling. The end result is that she figures it out, and usually by herself. She begins with feelings, then moves to talking and then to thinking. Eventually she develops the ability to do all three at the same time.

Because Wilma problem-solves out loud, Fred thinks he's either caused the problem or that she wants him to solve the problem. It's possible that he *could* fix it, but he shouldn't unless she requests a solution. Most women like Wilma just want their men to listen and reflect the fact that they've heard what the women are saying.

But Fred is not going to deal with his feelings in the same way, because for him they develop in another order. Often his feelings develop, then he moves to *action* and then to thinking. When an upset occurs, the immediate response is "Let's do something about it," and that helps him think it through. In time, he learns to feel, *act*, and think at the same time.

You'll notice that *talking* to resolve the problem *isn't* part of the formula for Fred. But it is for Wilma.

When a woman understands this, she doesn't have to be surprised when it occurs. She can accept it and even encourage the man to respond in this way and adapt some of her typical responses to more nearly match his.

Keep in mind that each side of the brain has, as it were, its own language. If a man is stronger in his left brain (in other words, if he's left-brain dominant) his language is going to be concerned with facts. It will tend to be logical and precise, as well as black and white.

True, some women have difficulty with feelings as well, but in the North American culture it's predominately the man who suffers with this crippling "disease," as counseling and seminars over the past two decades have thoroughly documented. Women are more familiar with the language of emotion than men. They've been encouraged as well as taught to express and value emotions. They've developed a language of emotions and feel comfortable with them.

Is *Emotional* Good or Bad?

What do you think of when you hear the word *emotional*? Is your first response a positive or a negative one? Has anyone ever called you *emotional*? Do you remember the last time it happened? What was the context? Was that person giving you a compliment? Did you respond by saying, "Thank you. I'm so pleased that you noticed"? Or did you take it as a criticism or put-down? Was the person who labeled your behavior *emotional* a man or a woman? Does the gender of the person using the word *emotional* affect how you interpret its meaning?

When most people use the word *emotional*, they're referring to someone's behavior: "Stop being so emotional." "You are starting to sound emotional." It's also used to describe an enduring characteristic of a person: "She's just an emotional person."

The word *emotional* doesn't seem to have any clear definition. Its definition is influenced by the behavior of the person who is being described and the intentions of the one who is doing the labeling. Being emotional has something to do with the frequency, intensity, duration, and appropriateness of a response.

What is clear is that the label *emotional* is mostly used in a negative context. It's often used in an attempt to influence or control a person's behavior. An emotional person is usually considered irresponsible, immature, and irrational. We've done a word-association test with several women's groups for the word *emotional*, and some of the words they find most frequently associated with it include *out of control, immature, irresponsible, irrational,* and *childish.*

WHAT'S UP WITH HOW WE FEEL

Why don't things always run smoothly with our emotions? Because both men and women sometimes create barriers against their own feelings and turn against involvement with others who are freer to express their feelings. The language difference is uncomfortable. We wall ourselves in and others out and so become self-contained hermits or prisoners, even in the presence of others.[2]

Feelings make up one-third of our awareness. Our intellect and our will (or determination) make up the other two-thirds. Some people choose to live functioning on two cylinders rather than on all three, which puts a strain on the vehicle. The other two can't make up for our emotional silence and insensitivity. Feelings are guideposts as we travel through life. We send and receive signals for support, love, nurturing, and protection—all our basic needs. Feelings are there to inform us, not to threaten us. But it's difficult for men. Here's what some have said about this in seminar groups:

The big issue we're always taking hits about are emotions, feelings, or whatever you call them. There's confusion here for both men and women. We *are* emotional beings. We are not as insensitive as we are stereotyped to be, but we have difficulty moving from the logical/linear side of the mind to the emotional—that is, if we are left-brained males—and not all of us are left brained either.

We do need to be emotionally connected to the women in our lives. Women tend to label us as loners. It's not true for all of us—alone at times, yes, but not loners.

There are reasons why we keep our feelings to ourselves. One is to spare and shelter our wives from pain; the other is we fear we'll be told what to do or interrogated about what we have shared. That won't work!

I'd say many women don't understand the reality and depth of emotional pain we men feel, especially when it's related to feelings of inadequacy imposed by society's markings of a real man—financial success, sexual potency, physical stature, competency, etc. I wonder if the average wife knows how much her husband needs her support, admiration and affirmation. I wonder. . . .

Many of us would like to communicate with our wives as intimately as they communicate with their friends. But we find it difficult. Who will help us learn? We receive few offers—only complaints.

Dr. Ken Druck has suggested some ways in which men especially tend to appear emotionally unaffected and in control:

• Men rationalize a course of inaction by telling themselves, *What good is it going to do to talk about it? That's not going to change anything!*

• Men worry and worry internally but never face what they really feel.

• Men escape into new roles or hide behind old ones.

• Men take the attitude that the "feelings" will pass and shrug them off as unimportant.

• Men keep busy, especially with work.

• Men change one feeling into another—becoming angry instead of experiencing hurt or fear.

• Men deny the feeling outright.

• Men put feelings on hold—put them in the file drawer and tend to forget what they were classified under.

• Men confront feelings with drugs and alcohol.

• Men are excellent surgeons. They create a "thinking bypass" to replace feelings with thought and logic.

• Men tend to let women do their feeling for them.

• Men sometimes avoid situations and people who elicit certain feelings in them.

• Some men get sick or behave carelessly and hurt themselves so they have a reason to justify their feelings.[3]

People who are unaware of their emotions may also be out of touch with the sources of tension that overstimulate certain systems of the body. These can produce or aggravate such physical symptoms as ulcers, colitis, asthma, skin rashes, headaches, muscular aches, and tics. The bottom line in this: how a person deals with his emotions and feelings determines to a great extent his physical, mental, and interpersonal health.

What would help a husband share his feelings?

THE KEYS TO MEN'S EMOTIONS

Sharing feelings presents a risk with a bottomless abyss waiting for us if we slip. Men have expressed what hinders them from sharing and what would help them. Listen to them:

I'll tell you what would help me share more with my wife. For me to open up with her, there has to be no risk. I can be honest but I don't want to be hassled. I don't want to be judged for what I share, and I want to share for as long as I want—and then have the freedom to quit when I need to.

My wife is an expert on what is a "feeling" and what isn't a "feeling." I have tried to tell her what is going on inside of me and she says, "But that's not a feeling." Where is this book she uses to tell herself what is a feeling and what isn't? I feel like giving up if I'm never going to get it right.

Yeah, I shared my feelings. And you know what happened? I opened up about work and my frustrations and she claimed I just wanted sympathy and attention. I tried to show her some love and attention and she said, "You must want something, like sex. You've got some other motive in mind." I try to be what she wants and I get criticized because my motives are suspect.

My wife tells me what I ought to be feeling. If she feels a certain way, I should feel the same way. If we watch a gripping movie, she wants me to feel what she feels. When she cries at church, she says, "But didn't you feel the same way? How could you not feel that way about what was shared?" Women's feelings are not the only right feelings, and if I have to feel the same way, it will never work. Can't two people in the same situation feel differently and with a different intensity—and even express it differently?

GETTING COMFORTABLE WITH COMMUNICATING FEELINGS

Many men choke when it comes to sharing tender, caring feelings with others. They're not cruel, insensitive, noncaring people; they merely find it impossible to communicate their inner reservoir of emotional expression.

I've talked with such men. I remember one in particular who said, "I was so proud of my wife the other day. She has been taking some art lessons and finished her painting. It was displayed in the window of the artist's studio and two people wanted to buy it for an incredible amount of money! I don't know that much about art, but I thought it was great and was really feeling good about her success."

I replied, "That's great. How much of what you just shared with me did you tell her?"

He looked at me and said, "Well, I'm sure she knows how proud I am of her."

I replied, "How? How would she know that? Did you tell her what you told me? Did you tell her you were proud of her? Did you tell her you were feeling good about her success? Did you tell her you thought her art was great?"

He waited pensively, then looked up at me and said, "No, I guess I didn't. It would make a difference, wouldn't it?"

I replied, "Yes, it could change her perception of you to that of a caring person if you would let her in on those feelings."

What can a man do who has never learned to share his feelings? Several steps can make a difference.

First, never compare your abilities to express feelings with a woman's. Comparison may keep you from trying. You listen to women share and then you think, *Forget it! I couldn't share like that, nor do I want to!* No one is suggesting that you share the way a woman does, but you can develop the untapped potential for expressing your unmasked feelings and developing intimacy.

Second, realize that becoming aware of and sharing your feelings offer you a multitude of life-changing benefits. As a result, you will relate significantly better to a wider range of people, including feelings-oriented men and women. More people will listen to you and respond to you. Psychologically and physically, you will be giving your wife one of the most desired gifts you could ever give her—real intimacy! And you will set a great model for your children.

Third, listen to how others describe and share their feelings. Learn from them. Make a list of feeling words and memorize them. Expand other areas of your vocabulary as well, and use these new terms in sentences within your mind until you become comfortable with them. Some men I know have practiced out loud to accustom themselves to hearing the spoken words. (Chapter 8 offered some; see more in the table at the end of this chapter for another list of "feeling" words.)

Fourth, learn to use word pictures to describe what is going on inside of you. Instead of just saying "I had a hard day," you could describe your day like this: "At times today it was so rough and frustrating. I felt as if I were trying to push an elephant out of the way and finally it sat on me!" Or "At one point today, it seemed as if it was raining on everything I tried. I was really discouraged!"

Fifth, try writing out what is going on inside of you. If you have a habit of saying "I think," you could change it to "I feel" or "I felt" or "my inner reaction was."

Sixth, let your wife know that one of your goals is to learn to share your feelings, and that you need her help and support. The following suggestions will alleviate misunderstanding and help to enlist the support you need:

• Explain that it will be difficult for you, and that it would be helpful to you if she recognized your progress.

• Let her know that sometimes the way you share may not seem clear and may differ from the way she would share in response to the same experience. Let her know that you want to understand. Tell her it would be best if she just asked a simple clarifying question rather than giving you correction.

• Give yourself permission to process your thoughts. There will be times when you need first to think through what you are feeling to access your emotions. If there is silence, don't fill it in with words or questions.

• Ask for understanding and grace. Tell her that when feelings are shared, you don't want to hear judgments or criticisms.

• Ask for confidentiality when personal feelings are shared. Let her know that you would prefer that she not pass these discussions along to others.

• State clearly what you want. If you don't want to *discuss* your feelings but simply *state* them, let your wife know. If you don't want to talk about your feelings at the time or even later, let her know that too. She is not a mind reader.

• When your wife wants to discuss her feelings, find a time that is agreeable for both of you. Turn off the TV, don't answer the phone, lock up the kids, put down the newspaper, put the dog in the refrigerator—and now that I've got your attention—look at her, listen, reflect her feelings by asking questions and clarifying what you heard, don't take what she says as a personal attack, and don't try to fix her.

How Women Can Express Their Feelings to Men

What is the best way for a woman to express her emotions to her husband—especially if he has difficulty coping with feelings?

Plan ahead and practice whenever possible. Share your feelings in small increments (piecemeal); don't dump them all at once. Emotional overloading tends to short-circuit and overwhelm men.

Ask your husband, "What's your reaction?" rather than "What are you feeling?"

Think of communicating with a man as speaking your native language to someone from another culture. I have learned to do this with my students from other countries, and they appreciate it.

Two wives shared with me how they helped their husbands with the communication process. One said to her spouse, "Honey, when I share my feelings with you it's difficult for me to edit. I will probably talk too much and dump a load of emotional stuff all over you. I just want you to know this in advance. You don't have to catch it all, just listen. If you want, I can repeat."

The other wife told her husband, "I appreciate you for sitting and listening to all this stuff. I'm not sure about all I just said. You probably feel the same way. Let's not talk now, but think about it and then sort through everything later. What do you think?" Both of these wives made communication easier for their husbands.

Keep in mind several cautions when a man expresses his feelings (which most women count as a gift):

First, never, but never, interrupt. I remember the first occasion I shared with my wife, Joyce, about the times when I had been depressed. I sat at the dining area table and Joyce stood thirty feet away with her back to me, washing the dishes. When I started sharing, she stopped what she was doing, came over, sat down, and listened. Not once did she interrupt or make a value judgment on what I was sharing. I felt safe.

Interruptions cause men to retreat and think, *Why bother sharing?* Sharing feelings takes more effort, energy, and concentration for men than it does for women. Men need to stay focused on one thing at a time. Interruptions throw men off course; and because men are goal conscious, they like to stay on course and complete the process.

Second, don't expect a man to remember how he felt about something weeks or months ago. Women have a large container for remembering feelings. One husband said that for men, it's more "like a cavern." But they seem to expand this feeling memory as the years go on.

FEELINGS ARE FRIENDS

Men and women need to quit viewing feelings as enemies and see them as allies. There are benefits of acknowledging and expressing feelings.

Feelings Motivate Us
They challenge us to do our best and assist us in some of our greatest accomplishments. Tapping into feelings is a tremendous energy source.

Feelings Create a Healthy Environment
Ignoring feelings depletes energy, whereas when we express them, the air is cleared and we move on in life. We do not become stuck with the excess baggage from the past. Expressing feelings is one of the best ways of reducing stress.

Feelings Are the Bridge to Other People
When we can trust our feelings and then in turn trust them to others, we build strong bonds of intimacy. Relating to others on the level of feelings means that we relate *with* them rather than *at* them.

Expressing Your Feelings Builds Self-Confidence
We tend to believe more in who we are and what we can do. We no longer have to live in fear of others discovering our feelings.

Feelings Help Us Make the Correct Decisions
Those who are in close touch with their feelings are more prepared to make difficult decisions and take important actions than those who are not.

Feelings Help to Heal Both Old and New Wounds
If you're hurt, you don't have to stay hurt. Feelings help us forgive others and also complete unfinished business.

Feelings and Their Expression Give Us Another Language
Sometimes just the facts won't do. Feelings give us more ways to communicate.[4]

WORDS TO FEEL WITH

How do we begin to develop the language of feelings?

The first step is develop a vocabulary of feeling words. One of the most practical ways to do this is to make a list of words you're already aware of and then take a resource such as *The Basic Book of Synonyms and Antonyms* and look up the various words. I looked up the word *fear* and found additional words such as *fright, dread, terror, alarm,* and *dismay.* The word *upset* can also be expressed as *disturb, agitate, fluster,* and *bother.*

Chapter 8 gave you some feeling words. Here are two more lists you can use as a resource. Once you have read through them, practice using them in sentences. Take one feeling and express it using some of the various words. When you share a response with someone else, attempt to use feeling words instead of expressing what you think. Remember that feelings are usually one- or two-word adjectives. If you give long dissertations such as "I feel that our government's position on Iran is. . . ." those are thoughts, not feelings.

Here is a list of eight different words with their amplification.

1. *Hate*	2. *Fear*	3. *Anger*	4. *Happiness*
dislike	fright	sore	joyful
bitter	terror	offended	enthusiastic
hateful	anxious	mad	merry
odious	misgivings	resentful	lucky
detest	concern	wrathful	fortunate
spiteful	harassed	hostile	pleased
aversion	dread	displeased	glad
despise	alarm	injured	satisfied
loathe	apprehension	vexed	contented
abominable	worry	torment	delighted

5. *Love*	6. *Disappointment*	7. *Sadness*	8. *Confusion*
affection	disturbed	tearful	mixed-up
loving	unhappy	grief	doubtful
amorous	unsatisfied	dejected	disorder
likable	frustrated	torment	bewilderment
tenderness	deluded	anguish	confounded
devotion	defeated	sorrow	disarray
attachment	hurt	unhappy	jumble
fondness	failure	gloomy	uncertain
passion	rejection	melancholy	perplexed
endearing	thwarted	mournful	embarrassment

Here's another list to help you learn the language of feelings. Notice there are words to describe your feelings when your wants are being satisfied and when they're not. In what situations would the words be appropriate, and when would they be inappropriate? With whom would you feel comfortable sharing these words? Check the feelings you can visualize yourself feeling and expressing. Select one and consider how you would express the word in a nonverbal manner.

When Wants Are Being Satisfied

absorbed	eager	grateful	peaceful
affection	elated	helpful	proud
alive	encouraged	inquisitive	radiant
amused	engrossed	inspired	refreshed
appreciation	enthusiastic	intense	relieved
astonished	excited	interested	secure
breathless	exhilarated	invigorated	spellbound
calm	expansive	jubilant	stimulated
cheerful	fascinated	keyed up	surprised
complacent	friendly	mellow	thrilled
concerned	fulfilled	merry	tranquil
confident	gleeful	moved	trust
curious	glowing	optimistic	wide awake
delighted	good-humored	overwhelmed	zestful

When Wants Are Not Being Satisfied

afraid	discouraged	hesitant	nettled
agitation	disgusted	horrible	passive
aloof	disheartened	hostile	perplexed
angry	dismayed	humdrum	provoked
animosity	disquieted	impatient	rancorous
annoyance	disturbed	inert	reluctant
anxious	downcast	infuriated	resentful
apprehensive	dread	insecure	restless
aversion	edgy	intense	scared
beat	embarrassed	irked	shaky
blah	exasperated	jealous	skeptical
bored	fatigued	jittery	sleepy
chagrined	fidgety	lassitude	sour
cold	frightened	let down	spiritless
confused	furious	listless	startled
cross	gloomy	lonely	suspicious
dejected	guilty	mean	thwarted

despondent	hate	miserable	troubled
detached	helpless	nervous	uneasy

It's important to learn your body's emotional signals. We all experience our emotions differently. For some, the feelings almost flood their bodies and overwhelm their rationality. Others need to first think about what they feel in order to become aware of the sensation. Still others experience their emotions first and then tune into their thoughts.

Begin to express your emotions with someone you trust. This is a person who isn't threatened by your expression and doesn't judge or criticize what you say. The person accepts you for who you are. When you do experience a feeling, share it as soon as possible, instead of letting it grow and even overwhelm you.

Once you begin to travel the road of expressing your feelings, you'll no longer want to take detours. Why? Because the benefits are worth all the effort.

Remember:

Being emotionally handicapped is common and can be overcome.

It takes less energy to experience and express our emotions than to hide them.

Feelings are our allies, not our enemies.

Build your vocabulary and then experiment sharing your new words.

By doing this, you will develop the flexibility to speak another language.

ENERGY BUILDERS

1. What do we mean by the word *emotion*? What is the role of emotions in our lives? Who has the most difficulty in expressing feelings? Why?

2. How do people put up barriers to emotions? Have you used any of these? How can you begin to tear down any walls you've built?

3. What is the proper role of feelings in a healthy life? How can you make them your allies instead of your enemies?

4. Have you developed the language of feelings? Practice using some new words if you need to. Does your language indicate that your wants have been satisfied? Are not satisfied?

5. How does your body react to emotions? Identify some of the signals it may be giving you.

6. What will you do this week with the information in this chapter? Describe how your communication will be different.

10

Storms of the Mind
STEP #10: MANAGE YOUR MIND-SET TOWARD YOUR MARRIAGE

I've never been in a hurricane and I never want to be. The tremendous force of the violent, swirling winds devastates everything in its path and leaves behind a trail of destruction. None of us will forget Katrina. I saw firsthand the results a month later. There were no words to describe the scene.

Within a hurricane, though, is a place called the *eye of the storm*. It's a place of such calm that you wouldn't even know about the fury going on elsewhere. But it's directly related to intense violent winds as they stem outward from this core.

It's not unlike what we see in many marriages. There's an eye of the storm in every person that can make or break any marriage. It's called our *thought life*, and it's marred. It has a bent toward negative thinking. We all experience storms of the mind.

Consider these examples. A husband comes home from work early and greets his wife with a hug and kiss. But in return she becomes angry and glares at him. Why?

A wife returns her husband's overdue books to the library and he becomes annoyed at her for doing so. Why?

A husband brags about his wife's cooking to a number of friends and she becomes furious at him for doing so. Why?

In each case, the spouse's positive action brought an unexpected reaction from his or her partner. The anticipated reaction was appreciation, not anger. What happened? Why the negative responses? Let's go back and look at the thoughts each spouse had in response to the positive overture.

In the case of the wife whose husband came home early, she thought, *Why did he come home at this time? Is he checking up on me? If there is anything undone, he'll criticize me, and I don't need that.*

The husband who has the overdue library books thought, *I was going to take those back. I'm capable of doing that. She's trying to point out that I'm not responsible. She doesn't trust me to follow through so she's going to jump in and do it herself.*

The wife who was praised for her cooking thought, *He never praises me that much at home. He's just using me to get attention for himself from his friends. He probably wants me to compliment him on something now. I wonder what they think about me now.*

In each case, these reactive thoughts just popped into their minds. We call this *self-talk*. Has something like this ever happened to you? Probably. It could be your thought was based on some past experience so, yes, there's a reason for it. But in each case, regardless of the intent and purpose of the spouse who did something positive, the reaction was such that it might limit a positive overture the next time. Most of us never think about that possibility.

What's Inside *Will* Come Out

So, what about you? Do you talk to yourself? Of course, it's all right to admit that you do. It doesn't mean that your chimney is missing a brick or your elevator doesn't go to the top floor. We *all* talk to ourselves. It's normal. We carry on inner dialogues all day long. Sometimes they're actual conversations, or they may simply be a series of beliefs we cling to and tell ourselves again and again. Our inner conversations reflect our beliefs and attitudes about ourselves, others, our experiences, the past, the future, and so on.

Think about this: what you express in your conversations with others is a reflection of the inner conversation you carry on with yourself. And how you behave toward others is determined by your inner conversation, not by their behaviors or responses. Your self-talk initiates and escalates most of your emotions, such as anger, depression, guilt, and worry.

Few people realize the tremendous power and effect of their inner dialogue. *Our internal thoughts determine what we do and say!* This means that what I've said in the previous chapters is dependent upon what's said in this chapter. You can attempt to listen with your ears and your eyes, pace another individual, match that person's tempo, inflection, and words, and even use words that reflect the person's vocabulary. But your inner dialogue will determine the effectiveness. Isn't that powerful?

Wouldn't it be fascinating to have a computer printout of your own inner conversation for just a day? You know what? We might be shocked to note some of the differences between what we say to ourselves *about ourselves* in our inner conversation and what we say to others in our outward conversation. Many talk to others quite differently from the way they talk to themselves.

What do I mean? Over the years I've discovered that many talk in a polite, concerned, interested, and objective manner to others, but they don't treat themselves with the same regard. They respond objectively to others but talk to themselves in an unrealistic, self-deprecating way that can bring on depression, low self-esteem, worry, and anger. These emotions in turn affect what we say to others and how objectively we listen and respond.

Many of our thoughts are automatic. They jump into our consciousnesses without any planning or prompting.

CHOOSING HOW WE RESPOND

We can all choose to react to what our spouses do with a negative interpretation, a negative assumption, suspicion over his or her intent, or in a guarded and defensive way. On the other hand, we could also respond at face value to what was said or done, give the benefit of the doubt, see it as a positive step, and show appreciation.

Your negative thoughts will generate anger, but if you correct them, the anger subsides.

One way to keep love alive in a relationship and to keep going in a positive direction is to be aware of your thoughts and beliefs about your relationship.[1] If the communication in your marriage could be better, look first at your thought life. If the way you behave toward each other needs improvement, look at your thought life. No matter what, look at your thought life.

The other day I went to the dictionary and looked up the word *slander*. Do you know what it means? It's the utterance in the presence of another person of a false statement or statements, damaging to a third person's character or reputation.[2] It dawned on me that some of our thoughts fall into that category. Many spouses commit slander in their minds. I've heard many such comments in my counseling office. Some of the thoughts we have about our own partners fall into the category of *character assassination* rather than *character adoration*. And this character-assassination style of thinking generates both conflict and distance in our marriage relationships.

Couples who have growing, fulfilling marriages have thought lives that are positive and healthy. What happens within the couple is a reflection of the inner workings of each person's mind and heart.

Many, however, struggle with defeatist beliefs. I've heard many of these beliefs over the years. But as some have worked at challenging these beliefs and becoming positive, I've also seen not only the persons change, but their spouses and marriages as well.

ROADBLOCKS TO BELIEF

Perhaps it would be helpful at this point for you to take few minutes and write out your thoughts about your marriage and your spouse, so you can become aware of whether these are thoughts that promote or hinder growth in your marriage:

1. My positive thoughts about my spouse are:

_____

_____

_____

2. My negative thoughts about my spouse are:

_____

_____

_____

3. Beliefs I have that help my marriage grow are:

_____

_____

_____

4. Beliefs I have that keep my marriage from growing are:

_____

_____

_____

Numerous patterns of thought can erode a marriage relationship. Let me take you back to the counseling office so you can hear some of the common beliefs that impede progress.

Assuming

One roadblock is assuming. Assumptions are usually negative. They portray the worst about another person. You make unfavorable judgments about your spouse. You hear him singing in another room and you think, *He's just doing that to irritate me. He knows that bothers me*. But you don't really know that. You can't determine another person's motive.

Overgeneralizing

This is one of the most bothersome thoughts and patterns of thinking, and it is difficult to change. Overgeneralizing includes statements such as "He never listens to me" or "She's always late" or "You never consider what I want." What's said may be plausible to you if you're upset over a few incidents, but these words are like insecticide that drifts across a field and kills the crops rather than just the weeds. A spouse hearing these statements usually gives up. When, in our eyes, our partners are *always* or *never*, we've condemned them and probably won't give them credit even when they do please us. And overgeneralizing, again, begins in our thought lives.

Magnifying

There are times when for one reason or another we may magnify. This is the tendency to enlarge the qualities of another person, usually in a *negative* way. When a situation seems out of control we may tend to think this way. A husband I knew wasn't the best when it came to spending and saving money. Once, when some checks bounced, his wife shared some of her thoughts with me: "He's such a spendthrift." "He does this constantly." "We won't have enough money for the bills this month." "If we're late on our house payment again, they'll foreclose." And finally, "We're going to lose our house and it's all because of him." I think you could imagine the ensuing conversation.

HOPELESSNESS BLOCKS BELIEF

I've heard many spouses say, "Nothing can change or improve our relationship." Now that is a defeatist belief. It will not only keep you from attempting anything, but it will cause you to look at your spouse as well as your marriage through a negative filter. It also becomes a self-fulfilling prophecy. It keeps you stuck.

Do you know what the results of this mind-set are? Let me give you several. And even if they don't fit you and your situation, they may fit someone you know.

With thoughts like this, you end up with a feeling of resignation: *I'll just have to learn to live with this.* You feel powerless and the downward spiral has started. You may begin to think less of yourself and that usually leads to thinking less of your spouse. And when that happens, your love and giving to your spouse begin to dry up.

I remember hearing one husband say, "I'm afraid my learning to live with it was the first step in learning to live without her." That's sad, since change and growth are possible in the majority of marriages I've seen.

I've also talked with spouses who end up feeling like martyrs. Unfortunately, martyrs usually let their partners know what they have to live with. They often dramatize the problems so well they could win an Oscar. And in time, another element emerges that destroys marriages—revenge. It may be hidden or blatant. All it does is set negatives in cement.

If you or anyone else believes that nothing can improve your marriage, test this belief. Don't let it decide your future. Challenge it. Look at the problems. Select one that appears to be the easiest to change.

One husband wanted just to be able to have discussions with his wife without the usual defensive arguments that seemed to erupt constantly. He and I actually had an enjoyable time brainstorming different ways he could stay out of the argument and eliminate his defensiveness:

1. He chose to believe that his wife wasn't out to get him or simply to argue with him out of spite. She might have some good ideas.

2. He committed himself *not* to interrupt her, *not* to argue or debate, and *not* to walk out on her.

3. He would respond to what she said by making such statements as: "Really," "That's interesting," "I hadn't considered that," "Tell me more," and "I'd like to think about that."

4. He also chose to think the following: *Even if this doesn't work the first time, I'll try it at least five times.*

5. He determined to thank her for each discussion, and when her response was even 5 percent less defensive, to compliment her for the way she responded.

Five weeks later, he called and said, "The fourth discussion was totally different. It's starting to work, Norm. You destroyed my belief that nothing can improve our relationship. There's hope now."

MORE DEFEATIST THOUGHTS

Would you like to hear another defeatist belief? Listen to this one: "My spouse won't cooperate and nothing can be done without her cooperation." Again, not true! We can't wait around for our spouses' responses or cooperation before taking positive steps. I've also heard, "But if I do something, he may resent it or it could discourage him and make him feel bad about himself." He could, but even if he did feel resentment or discouragement, you haven't forced him to respond in that way. And if you wait around for him to cooperate, you're just allowing his inactivity to control you. Is that what you want?

If you take the initiative, several positives are apt to occur: You won't feel so much like a victim. You'll be doing something positive. If you initiate change or respond in a new way, your spouse may respond differently if he or she sees the possibility of something new happening. What have you got to lose? Nothing. But you do have everything to gain.

Here's another defeatist attitude: *My partner is the most entrenched, stubborn person I know. He/She isn't capable of changing.* If you believe that, you'll act accordingly. He/She *won't* change, because you're not working to bring about change.

I believe everyone is capable of some change regardless of upbringing, personality, nationality, and even age. I've heard wives say, "He's German, you know, and those men don't change." These are myths. They're false beliefs that we buy into, empower, and perpetuate. The reason most spouses don't change is because we believe they can't. If we respond to them in ways that don't promote change, we could cripple their attempts to change by our own unbelief!

I've also talked to couples who felt if they tried to improve their marriages the relationships could grow worse. But if you don't put forth the effort, you'll never know. One wife told me, "It's tolerable now. It's not what I thought marriage would be, but it's better than nothing. And it's better than being alone." Unfortunately, a year later, she was alone.

If you work at discovering new information and approaches, there's as much possibility of the relationship improving as getting worse. And frequently a relationship may get worse before a couple finds the path to getting better. But it's better to be a risk taker than be paralyzed.

Some of the other defeatist thoughts I've encountered involve personal resistance to improving the relationship. Perhaps this has crossed your mind: *Why should I have to put forth all the work and effort to change?* My response is, "Why not? Why *not* you?" It shows maturity on your part and a desire for something positive. This step is a reflection of your inner character. Whether or not it has any impact on the relationship, wouldn't there be a sense of satisfaction on your part if you took this step? Not too many think about that.

Think of it this way: your partner may not have the same perception that you do of what's occurring in your relationship. I'm amazed at how often levels of satisfaction in a marriage can vary. One couple graphically expressed this verbally when I asked each the question, "On a scale of zero to ten, how satisfied are you with the marriage relationship?" The husband replied with a resounding, "Eight!" She said, "Three." That caused some discussion.

Many times I have seen this disparity in the responses to a marital assessment inventory that I have couples complete prior to coming for counseling. I ask them to answer these questions: "How committed are you to remaining in your relationship?" and "How committed do you think your spouse is to remaining in your relationship?" They respond to this on a scale of zero to ten. I don't know how many times I've seen one respond by judging his perception of his partner's commitment with an eight or nine, while in reality his partner's commitment, as evidenced by her own response, was only a two!

LABELS: FALSE ABSOLUTES

Another reason it's beneficial for you to take the initiative is because the two of you may differ in your motivation as well as in your ability to change. The spouse who's more optimistic or can become more optimistic, or the one experiencing the most pain, could be more motivated to take action. And both don't have to work at the relationship with the same degree of intensity.

Watch out for *crazy spouse labels*, such as:

My spouse
- is crazy.
- has a character disorder.
- is enmeshed with Mother.
- is an alcoholic.
- is a pervert.
- is sick.
- is impossible.
- is a stubborn _____.

My response to statements like these isn't what they expect. "If your spouse truly is crazy or has a character disorder, why should that stop you from working on the relationship? If he/she really is that way—and we don't know that for a fact—it might even be easier to get your partner to change." They'd never thought of it like that before. It's something to consider. Throw out undocumented, undiagnosed, and unreliable labels.[3]

Labels are false absolutes. We develop them to describe those who are different. We use them to justify ourselves and to keep us from thinking. If we used our minds constructively, we would be able to see both sides of a person. Labels limit our understanding of what is occurring in a marriage, for we see the label as the cause of the problem. Why look elsewhere?

Labels also keep us from looking at our part in the problem.

We use labels to avoid looking in the mirror for fear of what it will reflect. When you treat your spouse *as if* he or she is a certain way and possesses a particular quality, he or she may begin to act that way. Our negative expectations often become self-fulfilling prophecies and we end up cultivating what we don't want to grow.

Do you and your spouse label each other? Are the labels positive and motivating, or negative and debilitating? Are these generalizations attached to descriptions such as *always* or *never*? If you do label your spouse, perhaps you could learn to correct the label and, in your heart and mind, give him or her an opportunity to be different.[4]

AVOID VICTIM PHRASES AND CRIPPLING THOUGHTS

There's something else to consider: not only do your thoughts about your spouse impact your marriage, your thoughts about yourself will also affect your marriage because of how you limit yourself. When I work with couples I look for what I call *victim phrases*.

One phrase is "I can't." Do you say this to yourself? Words like these are prompted by some kind of unbelief, fear, or lack of hope. Any time you say, "I can't," you're saying you have no control over your life or your marriage. It takes no more effort to say, "It's worth a try" or "I'll try something new." This approach certainly has more potential. It shows you've become more of an encourager to yourself than a defeatist.

Victim phrases that can be marriage killers are "That's a problem" and "That's going to be hard." These are self-fulfilling prophecies. The next step is saying, "My spouse is a problem" or "It's hard to work on my marriage." Whenever you see what's occurring in life as a problem or a burden, you tend to become enmeshed in fear or even helplessness. Every obstacle brings with it an opportunity to learn, grow, and become a different person if you have the right attitude. Phrases such as "That's a challenge," "It's an opportunity to learn something new," or "Living with my spouse provides an opportunity for me to learn something new" mean you're on the right track, and it can work.

Another victim phrase is "I'll never be able to do anything about my life, my situation, my marriage, my spouse, etc." This is an indication of unconditional surrender to whatever is occurring in your life. In essence, you're saying, "I'm stuck in cement and won't ever be able to move." It doesn't give you an opportunity to make changes in your life. You could say, "I've never considered that before" or "I haven't tried that, but I'm willing to."

The question "Why is life . . . my marriage . . . my spouse this way?" is a fairly normal reaction to the disappointments of life. It's certainly normal at times to feel this way and even verbalize it. But choosing to remain there and stick with this attitude is crippling. I've seen some stuck there for life! It's not a pretty picture.

Victim phrases keep us prisoners in our own minds. By using them we limit growth. We limit change. We act out the rehearsal script of our minds for ourselves and others.

Sometimes thoughts like these are called *crippling thoughts* or even *hot thoughts*. They lead to feelings of hopelessness, anger, resentment, bitterness, futility, and depression. What you *feel*, you will *say*, directly or indirectly, and your partner will probably respond in such a way as to confirm your worst thoughts about him or her.

Many years ago a new jail was constructed in a small town in England. The builders said it was escape proof. Harry Houdini, the great escape artist known all over the world, was invited to come and test it. He had once boasted that he could escape from any jail, so naturally he accepted the invitation.

He entered the cell and the jailer closed the door behind him. Houdini listened to the sound of the key being slipped into the lock. The jailer then withdrew the key and left. Houdini took out his tools and started the process of working on that cell door. But nothing happened. It wasn't working out the way he expected. In fact, nothing that he'd done to unlock the door seemed to work. The hours passed. He was puzzled, because he had never failed to unlock any locked door. Finally, he admitted defeat. But when, in his exhaustion, he leaned against the door, it swung open. The jailer had put the key in but never locked it. The only place the door was locked was in his mind. Too often we're not much different.

The point I'm trying to make is this: thoughts like the ones we've discussed create problems. They don't solve them. Whenever you have such a thought or any negative thought for that matter, again, confront it. Challenge it. Debate with it. Change it. Ask yourself, *If I didn't have this thought, what's a better one I could have?* or *If I could change this negative thought into something positive, what would it be?* or *If someone else were to describe my partner, what would his or her description be?*

Negative thoughts and labeling never provide a full picture of your spouse. They're limited and slanted in one direction. Labels interfere with one of the ingredients most essential for a marriage to change, progress, and move forward. It's called *forgiveness*. Negative labels and thoughts block forgiveness. You have to see your spouse in a new light in order for forgiveness to occur. It's not easy to forgive a person you label as *callous, selfish, controlling, insensitive, manipulative, unbending, crazy*.

Sometimes I wonder whether we really know what forgiveness is. Forgiveness costs. It hurts. It doesn't always come easily. Forgiveness cannot be given out of fear, but only out of love and compassion. Forgiveness is an action that lets the other person know he or she is loved *in spite of*. Forgiveness is no longer allowing what has happened to poison you. Sometimes you feel as though forgiveness isn't deserved. But it never is.

That's what makes it forgiveness. It unfolds first as a decision to accept what you never thought would be acceptable. And negative thoughts and labels block that decision.

Consider these thoughts about forgiveness:

In forgiveness, you decide to give love to someone who has betrayed your love. You call forth your compassion, your wisdom, and your desire to be accepting of that person for who he or she is. You call forth your humanness and seek reunion in love and growth above all else.

Forgiveness is the changing of seasons. It provides a new context within which to nurture the relationship. The changing of the seasons allows you to let go of all that has been difficult to bear and begin again. When you forgive, you do not forget the season of cold completely, but neither do you shiver in its memory. The chill has subsided and has no more effect on the present than to remind you of how far you've come, how much you've grown, how truly you love and are loved.

When forgiveness becomes a part of your life, little resentment is left. Anger may not vanish immediately, but it will wither in time. The hot core of bitterness that was embedded firmly in your being burns no more.

Forgiveness comes first as a decision to act lovingly, even though you may feel justified to withhold your love.[5]

Forgiveness is a decision to wish another person well.

CHALLENGING THE NEGATIVE SIDE

Here is an example of how thoughts can put a damper on an otherwise enjoyable occasion, and how to interrupt the downhill slide and move it back to the enjoyable level.

June and her husband, Frank, went to a movie and afterward

Frank suggested they walk down to a restaurant and have a piece of pie. Let's look inside the mind of each as the conversation continued.

June's first thought was *Oh boy. He knows I've been trying to diet and lose weight. He's just thinking of himself as usual. You'd think he'd remember something as important as that.* June responded with an exasperated, "No, I'd rather just go home."

Frank thought, *Now what's wrong with her? We had a great time and now she's getting all bent out of shape. She sure goes up and down on her emotions.* Frank said a bit irritably, "Fine. Just forget it."

They each walked to the car in silence, but this time something new was beginning to take place. They were both learning to recognize how their thoughts had been feeding the way they responded to each other, and so each one, during the silence, was working on challenging his or her statements and destructive thoughts.

June began to think, *Well, maybe he just didn't think about it. After all, he's not the one on the diet, I am. And he's probably hungry. I could have a cup of decaf.* She also thought, *I guess I would prefer to go home and get some sleep. I've been overworked this month. I guess I must have snapped at him and I didn't need to. His request was innocent enough.*

At the same time Frank was thinking, *June has been pushing it at work recently. And it is 10:30. Maybe she's just tired and wants to go home.* He also thought, *We've worked out other disagreements. I think we can work this one out.*

June, who had calmed down by this time, said, "I didn't need to snap at you. I guess I was thinking about myself a bit too much. I guess I was looking forward to some rest. And I realize, too, that you could be hungry."

Storms are a part of life. We have no control over many of them, such as rain, tornados, and hurricanes. And they can be destructive. Storms of our minds can be just as destructive, but these we can control. It's a choice. Monitor your thoughts. If they build relationship, keep them. In fact, feed them! If they don't, evict them and then replace them. This can make all the difference. You can do this.

ENERGY BUILDERS

1. Look back over the negative thought patterns. Do you identify with any?
2. Describe how you can increase the positive thoughts about your spouse.
3. Can you think of any victim phrases you use?
4. How could forgiveness enhance your marriage?

11

You Can Choose What Works in Your Marriage
BONUS: CHOOSE THE SWEET LIFE

Years ago a couple came to see me with a particular problem. As we talked about what was occurring that brought them in, I discovered that this issue seemed to occur about every three to four years. I assumed that each time it happened they sought out a counselor, but that wasn't the case. This was the first time they had sought professional help.

I asked, "Is this a continuous issue in your marriage, or did you resolve it each time it happened?"

They said, "Oh, we were able to resolve it all the other times. But this time we thought we'd get some outside help."

I replied, "Well, I'm not sure you need me. If you were able to resolve it before, why don't you just do what you did before? It sounds to me as if it worked."

They looked at me with an expression that said, *Now, why didn't we think of that and save the money we're spending today?* Often this is the case. Look to see how you worked through issues before and do it again. If it worked once, it can work again. It can even be refined so it will work better the next time.

But you have to make up your mind to choose to find what worked.

CHOOSING THE SWEET LIFE

Life is full of choices. Some are difficult; others are easy. But everything goes back to a choice. We can choose to love or not to love. We can choose to be committed or not to be committed. We can choose to look for the best or for the worst.

If you have ever read about or observed various animals, you may have discerned the difference between the habits of buzzards and bees. Buzzards search for food by flying overhead and looking for dead animals. When they find the decaying animal, they move in to gorge. And the riper, the better. This is what they want. They have made their choice.

Honeybees, however, have different habits. They search for nectar that's sweet. They're quite discriminating as they fly through the various flowers in a garden. Some flowers just don't contain what the bees want, so they move on. They make a choice about where they settle in and feast. Both the bees and buzzards find what they are seeking. They make choices.

Couples make choices too. And I've seen couples who remind me of both the buzzards and the bees!

WHAT IS WORKING IN YOUR MARRIAGE?

The suggestions I'm going to give you in this chapter you may already have heard. But they need to be expressed again in this fashion. Why? It's simple: because they work. I've seen them help couples. They're not original. I draw from anywhere I can to discover what works, so I can pass it along to help others.

If I were to meet you and talk with you about your marriage,

I would ask you one question: "What's working?" A simple question, yet significant. If I held a marriage seminar with one hundred couples and asked everyone, "What are the problems and difficulties in your marriage?" what do you think would be the outcome after everyone shared? There would be a dark cloud of doom and despair. Everyone would probably leave discouraged and hopeless. I doubt if many would have benefited from their time together. I'm not suggesting that we overlook or ignore the problems. But there are better ways to solve them.

If I were to ask every couple, "What is working for you?" what a different atmosphere and outcome we would have following the meeting. Couples would have been encouraged and challenged by what they heard. They would have discovered new ways of revitalizing their own marriages.

Let's turn to sports for a minute. I enjoy baseball. Sometimes even the best of the hitters face a drought. They fall into what we call a *hitting slump*. And they try and try to break out of it. They consult with their batting coaches and analyze what they're doing wrong so they can get back on track. Many will get videos of themselves batting to see what they can learn. The videos they select will make the difference. Some look at videos when they're in a slump and watch their worst performances. They think if they focus on this they can learn what they're doing wrong and correct it. Unfortunately, this doesn't work very well.

Others select older videos that show them in a hitting streak and doing fantastic. They watch and observe what they were doing that worked. Soon they're able to go back to that level. They concentrated on what was working.

Marriage isn't all that different. The best step any couple can take is to focus on what is working. This is the best way to solve problems. I'm sure there are many times when you and your spouse get along. Can you describe specifically what you and your spouse do differently when you do get along? Think about it. Identify it.

I've heard many couples in counseling say, "We don't communicate." Often I ask about the times when they do communicate. I'm asking for the exceptions. Sometimes I have to be persistent and keep asking, especially when couples are full of pain and despair. At times the progress is slow, but soon I hear an exception to "We don't communicate."

One husband said, "Last Sunday after church we went out to lunch, just the two of us, and we talked all right. It wasn't bad." They were able to come up not only with this exception but several others. And what happened is that these exceptions began to counter the absolute belief that "We can't communicate." This is the beginning step to building a sense of hope and optimism. The exceptions begin to diminish the problems.

Too often, the longer a couple are married, the more each partner sees the other as incapable of changing. This can be in the realm of habits, behavior, or even attitudes. But as you talk about exceptions, you discover that under certain conditions and circumstances your partner is different. As one wife shared, "I used to believe that Jim wasn't interested in sharing his feelings with me. But when we go away on a trip for a few days, and especially when we get away from that darn phone, he seems to relax and get his mind off work. Those are the times when he does open up. I wish that somehow we could create those conditions more frequently." And in time they did. She discovered some changes were possible *given the right setting*.

Another benefit of bringing out exceptions is they might provide a road map showing the direction to take to increase the positives in their marriage. Discovering an exception might be the window a person or a couple needs to try a new path that will improve their relationship. It may help them develop a plan. So much of what happens in counseling is plan making. But the plan must be your own and individualized for your relationship.

Jim and Renee were a middle-aged couple with a marriage that had stagnated. Fortunately, they realized this and one day each stayed home from work. They went to a small restaurant that was out of the way and quiet. They told the waitress they needed a booth for several hours and would be eating both breakfast and lunch. They also promised a healthy tip. When I asked why they did this, Jim said, "We wanted to get out of the house into a neutral area, and the restaurant was cheaper than a hotel room. And being in public might have kept us from getting overly upset."

They both talked about how they wanted their marriage to be different twelve months from then. After they agreed on what they wanted, they identified three to five steps that both would take in order to reach their goal. They agreed to take one evening each month (on the fifteenth) to go out to dinner to measure progress and refine their plans. It worked, and it was much more economical than going to seek assistance from a marriage counselor.

A final benefit of looking at an exception is that it might enable you to discover a strength that will strengthen the relationship. It's a step of encouragement because it lets a couple know they've been doing something right after all.

Choosing Hope over Futility

It's far better to be people of hope rather than of despair. It's better to be people who confront obstacles and find a way to overcome them rather than to resign ourselves to a sense of futility.

It's strange, but I've found that some don't really want to discover the exceptions to the problem. Perhaps they don't want to hope, for fear they'll be disappointed. Some see the exceptions as just that: a rare exception that just happened. But we also struggle with selective remembering, and the painful experiences tend to lock in and persist. We emphasize failures instead of successes.

But it doesn't have to be this way. We can choose another direction. Let's consider the suggestions that numerous marriage counselors have offered to assist couples in having fulfilling relationships.

What Worked Back Then?

I've never worked with any couple that doesn't get along some of the time. We all get along well part of the time, and I realize for some it might be just 20 percent of the time. That's all right. It's enough. In order to have a lasting marriage, the first step is to discover what each of you is doing during the times you do get along. You can do this by yourself or with your partner. Brainstorm and figure out what each was doing before and during that time. Be sure to concentrate more on what *you* were doing than on what your partner was doing. This is the beginning point for any change. What were you thinking and feeling when you were getting along? Then plan to do more of it . . . regardless of what your partner does.

Sometimes people have mental blocks against identifying current expectations. If this is your problem, think back to a time when your marriage had some satisfying times. Often I'll have couples plot out charts of the history of the satisfaction level of their marriages. I ask them to identify the best experiences they've had since their marriages. "Best experiences" may have been times of just getting along. For some that's positive. And as we discuss these in detail, we talk about how we could create some of the same experiences right now in their marriage. Here is an example of the chart, and one husband's evaluation. The asterisk (*) indicates his level of satisfaction.

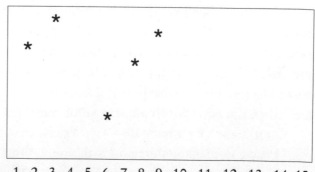

High
Satisfaction

Average
Satisfaction

Low
Satisfaction

1 2 3 4 5 6 7 8 9 10 11 12 13 14 15

Here is the husband's analysis of his chart:

Best Experiences
Two years—I felt loved and accepted by you. You had an interest in me and my work.
Three years—I think you needed me to help with Jimmy, and this was a good experience.
Six years—Seemed to communicate real well without fighting for a few years.
Eight years—Set aside ten minutes a day to connect.
Nine years—Had a week's vacation with no kids or in-laws; talked a lot and made love every day.

This is a good way to discover what worked in the past, to recall what we learned from it, and to put it into practice now.

Perhaps all of us as couples need to ask ourselves, "During the positive times in our marriage, what did we enjoy doing that we haven't been doing?" *Then do it.* Positive behaviors and responses create positive feelings

Creating Caring Behaviors

Over the years I have used a pattern for increasing positive behaviors for couples in both counseling and in seminars. I've talked about it and written about it before. I call these *caring behaviors* or *cherishing behaviors.*

Ask each other the question "What would you like me to do for you to show how much I care for you?" The answer must be positive, specific, and something that can be performed daily. The purpose of each action must be to increase positive behavior, not to decrease negative behavior.

"Please greet me with a hug and a kiss" is positive.

"Don't ignore me so much" is negative.

"Please line the children's bikes along the back wall of the garage when you come home" is more specific and thus better than "Please train the children to keep their bikes in the proper place."

Ted would like Sue to sit next to him on the sofa when they listen to the news after dinner. This is positive and specific. It's better than asking her to "stop being too preoccupied and distant" (a negative and overly general request).

Sue would like Jeff to kiss her good-bye when they part in the morning. This is positive and specific, which is different from "stop being so distant and cold" (a negative and overly general request).

Avoid making vague comments by writing down beforehand your answers to the question "What would you like me to do for you to show how much I care for you?"

The small, cherishing behaviors *must not concern past conflicts.* Your requests must not be old demands. That is, the requests must not concern any subject over which you have quarreled.

Again, the behaviors must be those that can be done on an everyday basis.

The behaviors must be minor ones—those that can be done easily.

These requests should, as much as possible, be something only your partner can fulfill. If they are things that a hired hand could perform, they may create problems. For example, if they are mostly task-oriented, like "wash the car," "take out the trash," "clean out the camper," "have dishes and house all cleaned up by the time I get home," they do not reflect intimacy and the cultivation of a personal relationship. Some better responses would be, "Ask me what excites me about my new job," or "Turn out the lights and let's sit holding hands and talking," or "Rub my back for a few minutes."

Each list should include fifteen to eighteen items. Listing as many as eighteen creates more interest and makes it easier to follow through with requests. When you give your list to each other, the only discussion you may carry on about the list is to ask for clarification if it is needed.

Now it will be your commitment to do at least two items each day on your spouse's caring list, whether or not he or she is doing any positive behaviors on your list.

Here are some suggestions for your "caring" list:

1. Say "hello" to me and kiss me in the morning when we wake up.
2. Say "good night" to me.
3. Sometimes bring me home a pretty flower or leaf.
4. Call me during the day and ask, "How's it going?"
5. Put a candle on the dinner table and turn off the light.
6. Hold me when we're watching TV.
7. Leave me a surprise note.
8. Take a shower or bath with me when the kids are gone.
9. Kiss or touch me when you leave for work.
10. Tell me about your best experience during the day.
11. Hold my hand in public.
12. Tell me I'm nice to be around.
13. Praise me in front of the kids.
14. Ask me how you can pray for me.

Many of the cherishing behaviors you request of your spouse may seem unimportant or even trivial. Some may be a bit embarrassing because they may seem artificial at first. That's all right. These small behaviors set the tone of the relationship. They are the primary building blocks for a fulfilling marriage. They establish an environment of positive expectations and change negative mind-sets.

When the lists are complete, exchange them with each other. Discuss the cherishing behaviors you have requested for each other. Don't be hesitant about telling your spouse how you would like to have the cherishing behaviors done for you. For example: "Ted, remember the way you used to bring me a flower when we were first married? You presented it to me when you met me at the door—after you had kissed me. It made me feel really loved."

During the discussion it's likely that both of you will think of a few more cherishing behaviors that you would enjoy receiving. Add them to the lists. The more the better, providing the lists are approximately equal in length.

The basic principle behind this approach is this: if couples will increase their positive actions toward one another, they will eventually crowd out and eliminate the negative. The consequences of behaving in a positive way override the negative. In addition, behaving in a loving, caring way will generate the habit of responding more positively and can build feelings of love. Choose at least two or three a day to give to your spouse.

How Much Is in the Bank?

Perhaps the following concept will illustrate the process in a different way. One of the metaphors used to describe a couple's interaction is that of a bank account. There are variations of this, but one is called a *Relationship Bank Account*.

As is true of any bank account, the balance in the Relationship Bank is in flux because of deposits. These could be a kind word or action or a very large gift of love. Withdrawals also vary. A minor disagreement could be small, but a major offense could drain the account. Zingers are definitely withdrawals, and so is defensiveness.

When you begin thinking of your relationship in this way, you can be more aware of deposits and attempted deposits as well as what constitutes a withdrawal. Naturally, the larger the balance, the healthier the relationship. And just like a monetary account, it's best to have sufficient reserves in your Relational Bank

Account. Unfortunately, many couples live with their balances at an overdrawn level.

There are two types of currencies in relational accounts—his and hers. Each may have a different valuation and could fluctuate from day to day. There's a difference in this type of bank—it's the "teller" or receiving person who sets the values of a deposit or withdrawal.

If there is a large balance in the account, a few small withdrawals don't impact the account that much. But if the balance is relatively small or hovers around zero, a small withdrawal is definitely felt. The ideal is to keep the deposits high and the withdrawals low. And each partner needs to enlighten the other as to what he or she perceives as a deposit or withdrawal. What is a deposit for you? For your spouse? What is a withdrawal for you? For your spouse? It may help you to discuss this concept for clarification.[1]

Sometimes I find couples might want changes that are reasonable but unattainable at first. Over the long haul, though, they can be accomplished. Trying for the unattainable breeds discouragement. It's better to work on very small attainable goals in order to eventually achieve the possible. Achieving a number of these small steps may in time resolve the major problem. It's better to spend time working on something you can achieve than something you can't.

Breaking Vicious Cycles

A different example of this is found in an approach that some marriage counselors use to help couples break free of the vicious cycle of reinforcing undesirable behaviors. There is a way to break a pattern on your own. It's not a matter of ignoring the behaviors but of making sure you're not helping to promote them anymore. It involves doing basically what a marriage counselor would have you do if you were in his or her office. But it does take cooperation from both the husband and wife.

The first step is to agree not to become defensive at whatever is written or said. The second is for each one to write out three problem behaviors each would like changed in his or her spouse. They should be listed one to three to indicate the level of importance.

The third step is to list your own reactions to this behavior. This is a very important part of the solution. The final step is to list desirable or positive behaviors you would like from your partner. Here is one wife's list:

I. Problem Behaviors of Spouse I'd Like Changed
A. I dislike his constant complaining. He complains about everything.
B. I dislike the way he forces his ideas and desires on me. He tries to shape me to conform to his expectations.
C. I dislike the way he never compliments me without qualifications.

II. My Reaction to These Behaviors
A. I tell him that that's the way it is and he can't do anything about it. Often, I say nothing and just keep it inside.
B. I am usually hurt by this and get angry and try to say something that will hurt him in return. I also tell him that I'm sorry that I'm not what he wants me to be.
C. I respond by usually saying nothing—just keeping it inside. Just some kind of recognition would really help.

III. Desirable or Positive Behaviors of Spouse
A. It's so nice when he gets excited about something we both can do.
B. I like it when he compliments me in front of other people.
C. I appreciate his doing the dishes.

This is a list from her husband:

I. Problem Behaviors of Spouse I'd Like Changed
   A. She has no desire for sex. She laughs when kissed—shows no sexual interest at all.
   B. She walks away from me when I'm talking to her. She usually tells me to shut up.
   C. She spends the little time we have together picking up things, taking showers, doing odd jobs, etc.

II. My Reaction to These Undesirable Behaviors
   A. My first reaction was to kiss her. When I found that this turned her off, I stopped. My trying to push her obviously annoyed her.
   B. I usually get mad and say things again to make sure she understands.
   C. I usually sit there, although sometimes I say something to her. It makes me feel as though her housework is more important than me.

III. Desirable or Positive Behaviors of Spouse
   A. She is a good cook.
   B. She works uncomplainingly.
   C. Keeps house clean.
   D. Very good mother to baby.
   E. Very organized.
   F. Dependable.
   G. Thoughtful about many things.

The next step is quite different from what some would expect. This entails keeping a weeklong record of the number of times problem behavior number three—the least threatening behavior—occurs. You do this not to blame or react to your spouse, but to help each other become more aware of your own reinforcing response to the behavior.

We begin with the least threatening behavior because it is easier to work out a mutual agreement with an easier problem. This should help any couple to proceed to the other more serious behaviors that need to be eliminated.

The way to eliminate a problem is to replace your reinforcing behaviors and increase the desired behaviors that your partner appreciates. Some partners verbally commit to each other that they will no longer respond the way they have, but let the problem behavior slide by. This takes patience and commitment, but . . . it works.[2]

Foolish Questions

Remember when you were a child and your parents came into the room to break up a fight between you and a sibling or another child? What do you remember saying? What do kids say today when this happens? "He [or she] started it." And it continues throughout our lives. We get into a disagreement with our spouses and we either think or say, "You started it!" And if we verbalize it, we usually frame it in the worst possible way by saying, "Why do you always have to start an argument?"

Fighting words. Ever said them? Ever heard them? "Why" is one of the worst ways to phrase a question. It puts the person on the defensive. Even if a person knew the answer to "why"—and often he doesn't—would he give the reason? And "always" is a gunpowder word. It's inflammatory. It incites a defensive posture, attitude, and response. And "have to" implies intent in a blaming way. You probably get the picture—bad phrasing of a question.

I don't think anyone is going to admit to starting the argument or fight anyway. Besides, regardless of who initiated it, would it continue if the other party didn't join in and participate? Not likely.

Instead of looking to see "who started it" what might happen if you concentrated more on how it ended? When you look at how disagreements end, you may find some solutions to use the next time and even shorten the disagreement. Learn from your solutions and successes. For some it's when they say things like:

I see your point of view.
I guess I've never considered that.
I've never thought about it that way before.
I think I understand.
You're right.
I'm willing to give it a try.[3]

One of the principles I've learned about crises and losses in life is that eventually as people recover, they are able to discover something positive or beneficial from the experience despite the pain and anguish. Sometimes it takes several months for a person to make the discovery.

In marriage disagreements or hassles, I think the discovery can be made earlier. The reason is we often don't look for it. When a problem arises, instead of constantly looking for the negative outcome, look to see what is constructive about it. It may be there but hidden or overlooked.

Some couples have discovered the following:

We're more patient with one another after we confront a problem or have a disagreement.
It takes me a while to see her point of view, but the only way I consider it is when we argue.
I don't like getting angry, but I do feel better when I don't keep it bottled up.
It's upsetting at the time, but we sure become more intimate afterward.

The Power of the Unpredictable

Another way to bring out positive change in a relationship is to do the unexpected. That is, doing something different when you know that what you're doing just isn't working. I learned about this in the early 1960s from a book I was reading in graduate school. The writer talked about it in relation to raising and disciplining children. Since I was a youth worker at the time, I wondered if it would work with teenagers—especially in large meetings.

Since most of us are predictable (including me), I began to think, *When some kid begins to act up and create a disturbance, how do I usually react? How does he expect me to respond?* Once I figured that out, I purposely did something different. Because they weren't expecting it, they couldn't defend against it. I found that it worked. Then as I moved into counseling couples I wondered if it would work in their relationships. I experimented. It did.

Some examples of the unpredictable things I have seen couples do are:

Instead of telling her husband not to get angry but to calm down (which never worked), a wife suggested that he needed to be angry and raise his voice. She pulled two chairs together and said, "Let's sit down and make it easier on ourselves." Interesting! He calmed down and sat down.

When a husband came in late occasionally because of traffic, instead of snapping at his wife when she complained that he should have called, he simply said, "Sorry" and gave her a tape that he had recorded in the car—complete with traffic noise—giving her a report every five minutes of where he was and how fast traffic was moving. There was no argument, and the next time he was late his wife had a different response.

Instead of telling her husband that he was yelling again (which he always denied), a wife turned on a tape recorder in plain view of her husband. This did the trick; the yelling stopped. Not only then but the next time when he started to yell, he saw the tape recorder and stopped.

On a humorous note, a husband shared with me that he hated

being predictable when he came into the house at night, so he thought up different ways of greeting each person when he arrived home. Some days he said he would crawl in the doggy door and surprise everyone. He might surprise them, but he could get shot in the process!

A therapist who is one of the leaders of this approach shared one of her own family experiences:

Knowing that a particular approach is entirely ineffective has no impact whatsoever on my choice of actions during subsequent crises. I find this to be a truly curious phenomenon. Consider what happened one evening at my house during dinnertime.

Since I rarely prepare a homemade meal for dinner (my husband is the gourmet cook), I expect punctuality (and appreciation) when I do. Although my husband is generally considerate about informing me of his schedule, he occasionally "forgets," returning home later than usual without a phone call to advise me of his plans. There seems to be an uncanny correlation between the extremely infrequent occasions I decide to prepare a meal and his "forgetting" to come home on time.

The sequence of events, when this occurs, is always the same. By the time he walks in, I have already tried calling several locations hoping to track him down. Dinner is ready and I mumble about the food getting cold. I suggest to my daughter that we begin without dad so that our food will still be hot. She senses my growing impatience. Later (what seems like years later) the door opens and I carefully plan my revenge—I will silently pout until he asks me, "What's wrong?" and then I will let him have it!

As he enters the room he greets us and seats himself, commenting about how good dinner smells. Then he cordially obliges by asking, "What's wrong?" and I jump at the opportunity to tell him. He defends himself and accuses me of being unreasonable. Things generally deteriorate from there. This particular plan of attack never works. I know this but my behavior belies this awareness.

However, something unusual happened one particular evening. The dinner scene was unfolding as usual when he walked through the door thirty minutes late. I was rehearsing to myself what I would say when he asked the million-dollar question. He predictably entered the room, said hello to us, sat down and began to eat. A couple of minutes passed and he did not inquire, "What's wrong?" "He's probably starving," I thought, reassuring myself that my attack was imminent. He then turned to my daughter and asked her how her day went in school. She launched into a ten-minute monologue consisting of the longest sentence I have ever heard. I thought she would never stop talking. After all, I was still waiting for my invitation to explode.

When she finally finished, instead of addressing me, my husband began to tell her some details of his day at work. She listened politely as I felt rage building inside: "What nerve, he didn't ask me why I am pouting!" I waited a while longer though I couldn't help but become mildly interested in the conversation. Without realizing it I found myself joining the discussion. The remainder of the meal was very pleasant.

When I realized what had happened I asked my husband why he decided to talk to our daughter instead of asking me about my silence. He replied, "You always tell your clients to do something different when they get stuck, but you never follow your own advice. I thought I would give it a shot." It's just awful to have your own weapons used against you![4]

Surprise Attacks

One of the most common conflicts I've heard is when a wife wants to share about her day with her husband, and the response is often not what she is looking for. Frequently, after about thirty seconds, when a husband realizes that this is going to take a while, he tunes back into the TV or begins rereading his newspaper.

Why does this happen so much? Simply because most men need to have a goal or a focal point. While a wife is sharing her feelings, and especially if she isn't talking in a linear fashion, a man is looking for the main point or bottom line. When he realizes it's going to take a while, he relaxes mentally and focuses on his viewing or reading. And many a man thinks he is still listening. Part of his mind is still with her. It's sort of scanning her words to see when she makes a point that calls for some response from him.

The typical—and worst—way a wife can respond is to say, "You're not listening!" This doesn't work for two good reasons. Many men heard this from their mothers, and now they feel they're being talked down to like a child again. They feel blamed. Second, they *do* hear their wives with a part of their minds. What they aren't doing is giving their full and individual attention—which is what wives really want.

Wives usually do one of two things, or both. They attack with the "You're not listening" statement and/or walk away hurt and upset. Neither works. Why not do the unpredictable? How? One way is to say what you really want and, if a husband is a bottom-line guy, put it in his language style. As one wife said, "Tom, when you begin looking at the newspaper again, I don't feel I have your full attention. That's what I really want from you. When you do I can share what I have to say much faster and more concisely. Then you can get back to your own reading or TV much quicker. And I'll feel good about it too." I think most men will not only hear this but understand.

Another wife did something totally different. When her husband turned away to read or look at the TV, she stopped, too, and just sat and waited. After a while he realized she had stopped talking and he looked up. She said, "Thank you. I need only three to five minutes more, and it helps me to have your full attention. Will that be all right with you?" This kind of approach usually gets the desired response. And whenever you get what you want, always thank the person.[5]

The Forgetfulness Fight

Another common issue in marriage is remembering and forgetting—one partner asks the other to do something and the partner forgets. The opportunity to attack presents itself and the partner who forgot responds in a defensive and protective way.

You've probably asked questions like "Did you pick up the dry cleaning?" (or "books at the library," "photos," "my prescription," "bread," "milk," etc.). That's a good question. It's positive. Much better than "I hope you didn't forget to . . ." or "I didn't see what I asked you to get and I was clear about how important it was. Did you forget again?"

Once you've asked in a positive way, respond in the same way if your spouse hasn't done it, with statements like "That's okay." "It's no problem." "Maybe we can get it tomorrow." If there is a time pressure, ask a question that solves a problem and can lead to a solution: "Honey, we need it tonight. Do you have any suggestions?" "Honey, we need it tonight. Do you want to run back for it? Or I could if you can take over this project." "Since we need it for this evening, I wonder if you could call one of the other couples to bring it."

Whatever you do, do something different if your usual response doesn't work.

ACCENTUATE THE POSITIVE

If you want your marriage to grow, focus on solutions, not just the problems. That's the message of this chapter. Switch the uses of your imagination to a positive direction rather than a negative focus. I think most people create complete full-length mental pictures of themselves engaging in martial combat with their spouses, and thus they are prone to make that a reality. When you use the same energy and time to focus your imagination and concentration on what's working as well as on the solution, you begin to expect that to happen. Act as if it is going to happen and talk as if it is going to be a reality.

This is nothing new. This procedure has been refined in the field of sports, especially tennis, racquetball, bobsledding, and skiing. In skiing, for example, on a downhill run, skiers see themselves making the precise moves at the right time as fast as possible. You actually see their bodies bob and weave as they go through the run in their minds.

I've used this rehearsal technique when playing racquetball, especially if I'm making bad shots and losing. When I concentrate on what I'm doing wrong, I continue to lose. But when I remember to concentrate on what works and what I will be doing with the next shot, I play better. It's as simple as that.

This is an important principle in your marriage too. Concentrate on what you will be doing either differently or positively. When you visualize your intent to be different or loving or accepting, you move toward that reality.

Perhaps it would be helpful to look at your marriage now, and consider what you like about your relationship that you would like to see continue. Talk together about what you can do to ensure that it does continue.

As you can see, everything suggested in this chapter is simple. Not at all profound. But over the years I've wondered why more couples don't follow these principles. As one husband put it,

"Norm, I just never thought about it like that before. Now that I do, it makes sense."

I think the potential for what can happen is summarized in this poem:

I will be with you
no matter what happens
to us and between us.
If you should become blind tomorrow,
I will be there.
If you achieve no success
and attain no status in our society,
I will be there.
When we argue and are angry,
as we inevitably will,
I will work to bring us together.
When we seem totally at odds
and neither of us is having needs fulfilled,
I will persist in trying to understand
and in trying to restore our relationship.
When our marriage seems utterly sterile
and going nowhere at all,
I will believe that it can work,
and I will want to work,
and I will do my part to make it work.
And when all is wonderful,
and we are happy,
I will rejoice over our life together,
and continue to strive
to keep our relationship growing and strong.[6]

Notes

CHAPTER 2: What Are You Trying to Say?

1. Matthew McKay, Martha Davis, and Patrick Fanning, *Messages* (Oakland, CA: New Harbinger Publications, 1983), 42.
2. Ibid., adapted, 70–78.

CHAPTER 4: Learning Your Partner's Language

1. *Webster's Collegiate Dictionary*, 10th ed. (Springfield, MO: Merriam-Webster, 2002).

CHAPTER 5: I Married an Alien

1. David Augsburger, *Sustaining Love* (Ventura, CA: Regal Books, 1988), 40.
2. Ibid., adapted, 39.
3. Ibid., 54, 56.

CHAPTER 6: Who's Listening?

1. Les and Leslie Parrott, *Love Talk* (Grand Rapids, MI: Zondervan, 2004), 121.
2. Lillian Glass, Ph.D., *Complete Idiot's Guide to Understanding Men and Women* (Indianapolis, IN: Alpha Books, 2000), adapted, 33.
3. John Ortberg, *Love Beyond Reason* (Grand Rapids, MI: Zondervan, 2000), adapted, 45.
4. Deborah Tannen, Ph.D., *You Just Don't Understand* (New York: William Morrow and Co., 1990), adapted, 188–192.

5. Aron T. Beck, *Love Is Never Enough* (New York: Harper and Row, 1988), adapted, 74–81.
6. Beverly Inman-Ebel, *Talk Is Not Cheap* (Austin, TX: Bard Press, 1999), adapted, 62–63.

CHAPTER 7: Women Speak, Men Speak
1. Michael McGill, *The McGill Report on Male Intimacy* (San Francisco: Harper and Row, 1985), 74.
2. Michael Gurian, *What Could He Be Thinking?* (New York: St. Martin's Press, 2003), 4.
3. Michael Gurian, *The Wonder of Boys* (New York: G.P. Putnam, 1996), adapted, 11–15.
4. Bill and Pam Farrel, *Men Are Like Waffles, Women Are Like Spaghetti* (Eugene, OR: Harvest House Publishers, 2001), 11.
5. Farrel, *Men Are Like Waffles*, adapted, 15–16.
6. Gurian, *Wonder of Boys*, adapted, 16–17.
7. Joe Tannenbaum, *Male and Female Realities* (San Marcos, CA: Robert Erdmann Publishing, 1990), adapted, 96–97.
8. Joan Shapiro, M.D., *Men: A Translation for Women* (New York: Avon Books, 1992), adapted, 71–84.
9. Tannenbaum, *Male and Female Realities*, adapted, 82, 40, and Jacquelyn Wonder and Priscilla Donovan, *Whole Brain Thinking* (New York: William Morrow and Company, 1984), adapted, 18–34.
10. Tannenbaum, *Male and Female Realities*, 90.
11. Gurian, *Wonder of Boys*, adapted, 23.
12. Deborah Tannen, Ph.D., *You Just Don't Understand* (New York: Morrow Publishing, 1990), adapted, 42, 77.
13. See *Transcultural Leadership, Empowering the Diverse Work Force* (Houston, TX: Gulf Publishing, 1993).
14. Judith C. Tingley, Ph.D., *Genderflex* (New York: Amacom, 1993), adapted, 16.
15. Ibid., adapted, 19.
16. Tannenbaum, *Male and Female Realities*, adapted, 77.

17. H. Norman Wright, *Communication: Key to Your Marriage* (Ventura, CA: Regal, 2000), adapted, 117–142.

CHAPTER 8: Translate and You'll Connect

1. Robert B. Diets, *Applications of Neuro-Linguistic Programming to Business Communications* (Cupertino, CA: Meta Publications, 1980), adapted, chapters 1, 2, 5. For another book on this subject, see Jerry Richardson, *The Magic of Rapport* (Cupertino, CA: Meta Publications), adapted, 75–98.

CHAPTER 9: Feelings

1. John Gray, *What Your Mother Couldn't Tell You and Your Father Didn't Know* (New York: HarperCollins, 1994), adapted, 90; and Joe Tannenbaum, *Male and Female Realities*, adapted, chapters 4–6. See also Gray's book *Mars and Venus Together Forever*, and his even more popular *Men Are from Mars and Women Are from Venus*, also from HarperCollins.
2. Ibid., adapted, 90–91.
3. Ken Druck with James C. Simmons, *The Secrets Men Keep* (New York: Doubleday & Co., 1985), adapted, 35–36.
4. Ibid., adapted, 39–40.

CHAPTER 10: Storms of the Mind

1. Beck, *Love Is Never Enough*, adapted, 108–110.
2. *Webster's New World Dictionary*, 3rd College ed. (New York: Simon & Schuster, 1994), 259.
3. Beck, *Love Is Never Enough*, adapted, 155–160.
4. Paul W. Coleman, *The Forgiving Marriage* (Chicago: Contemporary Books, 1989), adapted, 47–52.
5. Ibid., 22–23.

CHAPTER 11: You Can Choose What Works

1. Clifford Notarious and Howard Markman, *We Can Work It Out* (New York: G.P. Putnam's Sons, 1993), adapted, 70–73.

2. Alan S. Gurman and David G. Rice, *Couples in Conflict* (New York: Jason Aronson, Inc., 1975), adapted from "A Behavioral Exchange Model for Marital Counseling" by Alan F. Rappaport and Janet E. Harrel, 268–269.
3. Michelle Weiner-Davis, *Divorce Busting* (New York: Simon & Schuster, 1992), adapted, 126–128, 130–133.
4. Ibid., 148–149.
5. John Gray, *What Your Mother Couldn't Tell You*, adapted, 176–179.
6. Elizabeth Achtemeier, *The Committed Marriage* (Philadelphia: Westminster Press, 1976), 41.